The 60 Second Leader

T0373115

THE
60 SECOND
LEADER

Everything you need
to know about leadership, in
60 second bites

PHIL DOURADO

FREE!
Online leadership resource
www.60SecondLeader.com
when you buy this book

CAPSTONE

First published 2007
Capstone Publishing Ltd. (a Wiley Company)
The Atrium, Southern Gate, Chichester, PO19 8SQ, UK.
www.wileyeurope.com
Email (for orders and customer service enquires): cs-books@wiley.co.uk

Other Wiley Editorial Offices
John Wiley & Sons Inc., 111 River Street, Hoboken, NJ 07030, USA
Jossey-Bass, 989 Market Street, San Francisco, CA 94103–1741, USA
Wiley-VCH Verlag GmbH, Boschstr. 12, D-69469 Weinheim, Germany
John Wiley & Sons Australia Ltd, 42 McDougall Street, Milton, Queensland 4064, Australia
John Wiley & Sons (Asia) Pte Ltd, 2 Clementi Loop #02–01, Jin Xing Distripark, Singapore 129809
John Wiley & Sons Canada Ltd, 22 Worcester Road, Etobicoke, Ontario, Canada M9W 1L1
Wiley also publishes its books in a variety of electronic formats. Some content that appears in
print may not be available in electronic books.

ISBN 978-1-84112-745-3

Library of Congress Cataloging-in-Publication Data

Dourado, Phil.
  60 second leader : everything you need to know about leadership, in 60 second bites / Phil
Dourado.
    p. cm.
  Includes bibliographical references and index.
  ISBN 978-1-84112-745-3 (pbk. : alk. paper)
  1. Leadership. I. Title.
  HD57.7.D686 2007
  658.4'092–dc22

                                                                                          2007009230

Anniversary Logo Design: Richard J. Pacifico

Set in ITC New Baskerville by Sparks (www.sparks.co.uk)

ABOUT THE AUTHOR

Phil Dourado is a leadership consultant, speaker, author and journalist. His specialist area is helping large companies develop a global community of leaders who learn from each other online. He has written for a number of national newspapers and magazines, including *The Telegraph, The Independent, GQ, The Observer* and *The Business.* He edited two business-to-business journals before spending five years researching and defining great leadership practice as a director of the Inspired Leaders Network. This, his second book on leadership, grew out of research into distilling the essence of leadership for the *60 Second Leader* online development system. It follows the same principle of bite-size nuggets that can be digested quickly by busy leaders and put into action immediately to improve their leadership performance. Phil has an MA in history from Cambridge University and splits his time between consulting, researching, writing, parenting and caring for his wife, who has Huntington's disease. You can reach him through www.PhilDourado.com.

CONTENTS

The 60 Second Leader Tales

WHO THIS BOOK IS FOR

People in **formal leadership** positions are one type of leader. This book is for you. There are also many **informal leaders**, not recognized in the structure chart. This book is for you, too. Then there are **would-be leaders**, some of whom are being groomed as leaders by the organization you work for. This book is for you. Finally, and most interestingly, there are **should-be leaders**, the many potential leaders who do not even think of themselves as leadership material. This book is for them, too. If you know one, give them a copy. They are unlikely to pick it up themselves.

> 'Most leadership strategies are doomed to failure from the outset ... The first problem with all of the stuff that's out there about leadership is that **we haven't got a clue what we're talking about**. We use the word "leader" to mean "executive": The leader is the person at the top. That definition says that leadership is synonymous with a position. And if leadership is synonymous with a position, then it doesn't matter what a leader does. All that matters is where the leader sits. If you define a **leader** as an **executive**, then you absolutely deny everyone else in an organization the opportunity to be a leader.'
> Peter Senge

Introduction

THE 60 SECOND PHD IN LEADERSHIP

This book is a distillation of 30 essential elements of leadership into 60 second digestible chapters. There are also 30 true *60 Second Leader Tales* in between the chapters to help bring some of the leader learning points to life.

However, I don't want you to feel misled by the book title. So if you picked this book up expecting to find 'how to be a great leader in 60 seconds', then here it is:

THE 60 SECOND PHD IN LEADERSHIP

Think back to the best boss you ever had and the worst boss you ever had.

1   Make a list of all things done to you that you abhorred.
2   DON'T DO THEM TO OTHERS. EVER.
3   Make another list of things done to you that you loved.
4   DO THEM TO OTHERS. ALWAYS.

And you thought leadership was complicated.

Source: Dee Hock, founder of *Visa*. I first heard Hock's *60 Second PhD in Leadership* from Tom Peters, who uses it sometimes in his presentations.

So, if that is what you wanted – how to be a great leader in 60 seconds – the rest of this book is just gravy.

PERSONAL (SELF) LEADERSHIP

1. The 60 Second Leader and …

FAILURE

Forgive and remember. When Jack blew up the plant. The Tripping Point.

You probably don't think of yourself as a failure. But, you or so-called 'leaders' in your organization may find it a useful label to hang on others. Allocating blame when things go wrong is a long-standing convention for maintaining the myth of leader infallibility. It poisons your culture, as those below will follow the lead. Using the authority of position to cascade blame becomes the norm.

The best leaders adopt a different perspective on failure, encouraging a *forgive and remember* culture. Firstly, you separate failure from the person – it's an occurrence, not an inherent trait.* Secondly, you make it clear some failures are a desirable outcome of trying new things. Thirdly, you set in place practices for limiting damage when failure occurs and for capturing and sharing learning.

This last – sharing learning to prevent repetition of mistakes – is where most organizations still fail.

---

*The caveat is, of course, that even with the best recruitment methods you can end up with someone who repeats mistakes or just makes too many and has to be moved or leave.

> *The road to wisdom?*
> *Well, it's plain and simple to express:*
> *Err*
> *and err*
> *and err again*
> *but less*
> *and less*
> *and less*
> Piet Hein, Danish inventor and poet

Here's Jack Welch, the legendary CEO of General Electric, illustrating the importance of leaders tolerating failure, with an episode from his own past:

Kirsty Wark: I understand one of the first things you did at GE was blow up the plant you were working in and that it had a profound effect on you. Can you explain?

Jack Welch: I did accidentally blow up the plant, yes. I was about 25 and had been experimenting with a different mixture. There was an explosion. I was scared stiff when I went to the manager. But, he was mainly curious as to why I had done what I had done and what I had learnt from it. 'Would the process I was trying have worked?' is what interested him! That real encouragement to get it right rather than a punishment did have a profound effect on me, yes. [1]

Admit it: you would have fired him.

LIMITING THE DAMAGE OF FAILURE

Use pilots to limit the damage when trying new ways of working. The three principles of successful pilots are: think big; start small; scale fast.

MECHANISM FOR SPREADING LEARNING FROM MISTAKES

Jack Welch again:

> 'We celebrated mistakes at a management gathering with 1,000 people in the room. A manager would get up and say why the environmentally sensitive light bulb or whatever it was had failed ... then we'd give them $1,000 or a TV or something, depending on the scale of the thing. The point was to share the learning and get smarter as an organization.' [1]

ON THE OTHER HAND ...

You will hear again and again in leadership development circles the mantra 'learn from mistakes and failures'. But, in among the din of all that noisy received wisdom, I recently heard one voice point out that there is an uber-message about failure; a message that is more important than 'learn from your mistakes'. I heard **Bob Geldof** say this at the end of 2006:

> 'The Bob Dylan line always appealed to me: "There's no success like failure and failure is no success at all." It was a while before I understood it. Leaders need the ability to fail and then get up and go on. **It doesn't matter if you don't learn from the failure.** But it does matter that you get up and get on.'

USEFUL CONCEPT

The Tripping Point: [2] Refers to those moments in life where you land on your backside and suddenly realize, with blinding clarity, that you got it wrong. For great leaders at all levels in an organization, these are significant illumination points in life. The shock of failure sears into you, you learn, change and, as Geldof says above, get up and move on. And you show other people by your own example how to do it.

AND, FINALLY ... WHO'S THIS FAILURE?

(Thank you to Professor Aidan Halligan for sharing this with me):

1831 Failed in business

1832 Defeated for congress

1834 Failed in business

1835 Sweetheart died

1836 Had nervous breakdown

1838 Defeated for Congress

1843 Defeated for Congress

1846 Defeated for Congress

1848 Defeated for Congress

1855 Defeated for US Senate

1856 Defeated for Vice-President

1858 Defeated for US Senate

1860 Elected sixteenth President of the USA

Clue: Tall chap. Beard. Probably shouldn't have gone to the theatre. One of the most revered US Presidents in history.

SOURCES AND FURTHER READING

(1) Keynote interview, *European Conference on Customer Management,* London, 2004, organized by *www.ecsw.com.* The excerpts here are from my shorthand notes.

(2) I know, I wish I'd thought of it, too. But, I spotted the phrase 'The Tripping Point' in the book *Success Built to Last: Creating a Life That Matters,* Jerry Porras' follow-up to *Built To Last.*

Worth reading: *Why CEOs Fail,* David Dotlich, Peter Cairo *et al.* Eleven reasons leaders fail. Not just for CEOs, despite the title. My favourite is Number 4: '*Excessive Caution: The next decision you make may be your first …*'

A 60 Second Leader Tale: Leading by example

> *'Example is all in a leader. That's all leadership is.'*
> Aidan Halligan

Here's a true leader tale from Captain D. Michael Abrashoff, who turned around a poor-performing ship, USS *Benfold*, to make it, according to a number of measures, 'the best damn ship in the Navy'. That phrase became the strap line that Benfold sailors used to describe their own ship

'On Sunday afternoons, we had cookouts on the aft flight deck. One Sunday early in my command, I went back to observe. A long line of sailors stood waiting to get their lunch. My officers would cut to the head of the line to get their food, and then go up to the next deck to eat by themselves. The officers weren't bad people; they just didn't know any different. It's always been that way.

When I saw this, I decided to go to the end of the line. The officers were looking down, curious. They elected the supply officer to come talk to me.

"Captain," he said, looking worried, "you don't understand. You go to the head of the line."

"That's okay," I said …

I stood in line and got my food. Then I stayed on the lower deck and ate with the sailors. The officers became totally alert. You could almost hear the gears shifting in their heads.

The next weekend we had another cookout and, **without my saying a word to anyone** [*author's note:* my emphasis], the officers went to the end of the line. When they got their lunch, they stayed on the lower level and mingled with the sailors.

Given the Navy's basically classist society, to say that the fraternal scene on the flight deck was unusual would be an understatement. To me, it felt right …

As Captain I was charged with enforcing 225 years of accumulated Navy regulations, policies, and procedures. But every last one was up for negotiation whenever my people came up with better ways of doing things. To facilitate that I had to encourage the crew to take initiative – and make sure the officers welcomed it. And that meant they would have to get to know one another as people. They would have to respect one another, and from that would come trust.'

Source: *It's Your Ship: Management techniques from the best damn ship in the Navy*, by Captain D. Michael Abrashoff, an instinctive, largely self-taught leader. This book is packed full of practical lessons for challenging hierarchy and improving performance through inspired leadership.

2. The 60 Second Leader and …

INTUITION

How George Soros makes investment decisions and how Kjell Nordstrom's dad finds fish.

There's a great distrust of instinct and intuition in business leadership today. Analysts, investors and regulators want to see the solid ground on which your decisions are built. Post-dotcom bubble, post-*Enron*, post-*Worldcom*, people are wary of anything that may not be grounded in reality (or legality, come to that).

Professor **Bob Sutton** of *Stanford University* says, as part of the promotion of facts over intuition, 'Organizations that rely on facts rather than intuition can outperform the competition'. [1] Now I have a lot of time for the thinking of Bob Sutton, but the problem with this particular thinking is that *intuition and facts are not mutually exclusive*. Here are two examples of the power of intuition as an expression of **tacit knowledge** – things you know in your bones but can't always put into words.

The first is from **Malcolm Gladwell**:

> 'My father will sit down and give you theories to explain why he does this or that,' the son of the billionaire investor George Soros has said. 'But I remember seeing it as a kid and thinking, "At least half of this is bull." I mean, you know the reason he changes his position on the market or whatever? It is because his back starts killing him. He literally goes into spasm and it's this early warning sign.' [2]

PLOUGHED-IN KNOWLEDGE

Instinct and intuition should not be lumped in with narrowness of thinking and selective use of evidence. Often intuition draws not on hopes, fears and prejudice, but on the kind of deep knowledge that it is difficult or impossible to articulate and evidence in a report because it is implicit. Intuition grows from ploughed-in knowledge.

Here's more, er, evidence in favour of intuition. It's a story the economist **Kjell Nordstrom** told me:

> *'My father's a fisherman. He has been all his life. Occasionally he takes me out fishing in his boat. After a while, I'll say, "This looks like a good spot. Let's stop here and fish." My father will just smile and say "Not today. Today the fish are over there," and point a mile or two to the west. And he is nearly always right. I have given up asking how he knows. He looks at the sky. He feels the wind. He watches the waves and senses the currents. He just knows where the fish are.'*

Facts and intuition are *false opposites*. Leaders should listen to their intuition and instincts and allow others to do the same because they are subconscious, fast ways of processing, aggregating and then accessing evidence to reach a swift conclusion. Trust your gut. And make it clear to your people that you trust them to use theirs.

But balance in all things. Leaders need more of both – a clear-eyed focus on the relevant facts and evidence, rather than evidence that promotes a particular agenda or perspective, **PLUS** more reliance on individual and collective instinct. Collective instinct? See the next chapter, *Decisions*, for an explanation.

USEFUL CONCEPT

Thin slicing: Malcolm Gladwell [2] says we make snap decisions all the time, apparently based on tiny slivers of information. It's called thin slicing. He gives the example of a woman at a speed-dating event who says of one failed encounter, 'He lost me at "Hello".' These fast decisions are often better than the outcomes of long, deliberative reasoning processes. But, they can also be wrong.

SOURCES AND FURTHER READING

(1) *Hard Facts, Dangerous Half Truths and Total Nonsense*, Bob Sutton and Jeffrey Pfeffer. Partly-inspired by the growth in recent years of the Evidence-Based Medicine movement in healthcare, Sutton and Pfeffer argue that the approach should be carried over into how organizations are run. Up to a point, gentlemen.

(2) *Blink: The power of thinking without thinking*, Malcolm Gladwell. Intuition and instinct are by no means always right. But, they are powerful tools in your decision-making, explains Gladwell.

A 60 Second Leader Tale: Branson and gut leadership … or how an unanswered phone led to the birth of Virgin Atlantic

> *'I can make up my mind … in sixty seconds.'*
> Richard Branson

In this true leader tale, Richard Branson says trusting your gut can be more powerful than any amount of reports:

'I can make up my mind about people and ideas in sixty seconds. I rely more on gut instinct than thick reports. I knew within a minute that this was for me – a 1984 proposal from a young American lawyer to invest in a new airline.

It was a very bold step, but worth it. I decided to look into it. I had to work out in my own mind what the risks were.

There was already a popular airline that sold cheap fares across the Atlantic. It was called *People Express*. I tried to call them. It seemed everyone must have wanted to fly, as their lines were busy. I tried all day but I couldn't get through.

I knew I could run an airline better than that. I spent a weekend thinking it over. By Sunday evening I had made up my mind. I would be bold. I would *just do it.*

On Monday, I called Boeing. I asked how much it would cost to rent a jumbo jet for a year. They were surprised, but they listened to me. By the end of the call we had worked out a good price. I felt I had done enough research.'

At the time, *Virgin Music* was highly profitable. Branson worked out that the money to start an airline was less than a third of a year's profits from *Virgin Music*. 'It was a lot, but not too much. Even if we lost it all, we would survive,' he said. 'I always encourage people to be bold, but not to gamble.'

Source: *Screw It, Let's Do It*, Branson's short-form autobiography, which you can read in less than an hour. It's a distillation of his longer book *Losing My Virginity*. Both are highly recommended.

3. The 60 Second Leader and ...

DECISIONS

Intuition and decisions. Not what but when. Decision markets.

> *'The more important a decision, the more important it is that it not be left in the hands of a single person.'*
> James Surowiecki [1]

Paul Van Riper, a retired Marine Lieutenant General, is famous in military circles for out-thinking and beating the Pentagon's battlefield decision support system during war game exercises. He once tried an experiment to test his theory that there were better ways to make decisions than the military's top-down approach. Van Riper got a group of Marines, trained in the military's rational decision-making techniques, to compete in a trading simulation game with traders on the New York Mercantile Exchange. The instinctive traders wiped the floor with the methodical Marines. When they tried the same with war games back at the Marines' HQ ... the traders wiped the floor with the Marines there, too. [2]

LESS IS MORE

The lesson Van Riper learned is that, in fast-moving situations, a decision based on 80 per cent of the information plus informed intuition is often far better than waiting for a 100 per cent informed solution. By the time your perfect information has been gathered, the world has moved on. 'Decisions don't wait; investment decisions or personal decisions don't wait for that picture to be clarified,' as **Andy Grove**, employee Number 3 of *Intel* put it. [3]

ON THE OTHER HAND ...

Leaders often assume they have to make decisions quickly, that lingering over decision-making indicates weakness. This is particularly true of leaders in new positions who have read all the literature telling them to make an impact in the first 90 days and who want to stamp their mark as a decisive leader. But, former New York Mayor **Rudy Giuliani** advises us not to make decisions until you have to. The ability to reflect and ponder outcomes before acting is a sign of strength, not weakness, he stresses:

> 'One of the trickiest elements of decision-making is working out not what, but when. Regardless of how much time exists before a decision must be made, I never make up my mind until I have to. Faced with any important decision, I always envision how each alternative will play out before I make it. During this process, I'm not afraid to change my mind a few times. Many are tempted to decide an issue simply to end the discomfort of indecision. However, the longer you have to make a decision, the more mature and well-reasoned that decision should be.' [4]

GROUP DECISION-MAKING

The very phrase 'group decision-making' probably has you reaching for the Scotch and shaking your head in despair. The objections are well rehearsed: nobody built a statue to a committee, consensus decisions are inherently weak, 'group think' is slow and herd-like. And yet, and yet ... the received wisdom on this may now be past its sell-by date. The Boeing 777 jet airliner emerged from an exercise in group decision-making to help identify where *Boeing* should go next. See the work on participative leadership through **critical mass interventions** described later in this book.

DECISION MARKETS

Using 'smart groups' as a decision-support mechanism brings the power of the market into your organization. *Hewlett-Packard* and *Innocentive*, a spin-off of *Eli Lilley*, have both experimented with the smart groups principle to cre-

ate internal decision markets, tasked with predicting which products would win out in the marketplace. The markets – made up of a diverse group of employees from across each business – out-performed the decisions made by the companies' leaders.

Smart groups do not consist of particularly smart or expert individuals. They are a cross-section of people. **James Surowiecki** [1] has explained the four conditions that allow a group to be smart:

Smart groups beat individual decisions if they have

1 **Diversity of opinion** (each person should have some private information, even if it's just an eccentric interpretation of the known facts)

2 **Independence** (people's opinions are not determined by the opinions of those around them)

3 **Decentralization** (people are able to specialize and draw on local knowledge)

4 **Aggregation** (some mechanism exists for turning private judgements into collective decision).

The mathematical principle is simple, says Surowiecki: 'Ask a hundred people to answer a question or solve a problem and the average answer will often be at least as good as the answer of the smartest member. With most things, the average is mediocrity. With decision-making, it's often excellence.'

USEFUL CONCEPT

OODA loops: Stands for Observe, Orientate, Decide, Act. A decision-making system developed by fighter pilot John Boyd. If you are steeped in a fast-changing environment, rather than distant from it, you 'wick up' information like an oil lamp and your resulting fast decision-making is more likely to be right. [5] Yet few top leaders spend a significant amount of time out where the action is, absorbing information through their pores, instead of through reports.

SOURCES AND FURTHER READING

(1) *The Wisdom of Crowds: Why the Many Are Smarter Than the Few*, James Surowiecki. Especially powerful are the last few pages of Chapter 10, which give detail of how the *HP* and *Innocentive* internal decision markets worked.

(2) *Sources of Power*, Gary Klein's classic book on decision-making, with a slightly misleading title. Klein studied nurses, fire fighters and others who make fast decisions under pressure.

(3) 'Decisions Don't Wait', a paper in the *Harvard Management Update*, January 2003, in which Clayton Christensen and other Harvard faculty members interview Andy Grove of Intel.

(4) *Leadership*, Rudy Giuliani.

(5) *Boyd: The fighter pilot who changed the art of war*, Robert Coram's biography of the fascinating John Boyd.

A 60 Second Leader Tale: Unexpected leaders

> *'A leader is the one who climbs the tallest tree, surveys the entire situation, and yells: "Wrong jungle!"'*
> Stephen Covey

Don't look for leadership just at the top of the tree. Listen to leadership wherever it is expressed. Particularly, allow it to flourish in unexpected places. Here's an example ...

Tilly, who was ten at the time, was on the beach at Phuket, Thailand, with her family. It was December 2004. She noticed the sea looked odd. It was foaming, like the head of a beer, all across the surface instead of just where the waves had broken. 'Bad sea day', as in 'bad hair day', she and her mum joked together.

'Then I suddenly had a vision in my head of the video we watched in a geography lesson of the sea in Hawaii before a tsunami. It was exactly the same,' Tilly said later. At first her mum didn't get it when Tilly told her, as if in a scene from the film *Jaws*, that they had to get everyone out of the water. So certain was Tilly of her recollection and of what was about to happen that she began shouting to get her parents to listen.

Instead of telling her to calm down and be quiet, her parents were focussed by Tilly's sense of urgency, and paid her their full attention. They quickly agreed to get the rest of the family off the beach, then persuaded the lifeguards to start getting people out of the sea. They warned as many people as possible and then turned and ran when it became obvious Tilly was right about what was coming. Listening to a 10-year-old girl with a powerful story to tell saved their lives and the lives of many others.

So, the one who climbs the tallest tree and sees the bigger picture, as Stephen Covey puts it, doesn't have to be the person who heads the organization. Sometimes people at the front line, maybe in a relatively junior position, have a clearer view of where the organization is going wrong and, in this case, of a disaster that is about to strike.

What allowed Tilly to become a leader in this situation was a combination of her learning, her confidence in her own judgement, her urgent sense that she could and should make a difference, her concern and sense of responsibility for other people, and the readiness of her family to listen to her, trust her and ultimately be led by her.

Does your organization (and that includes you) create that same set of circumstances (culture) to allow people at all levels to step up and take the lead when they need to? And when you see the need to take the lead, no matter what your position in the hierarchy, do you step forward and speak up?

Author's Note: It has been pointed out to me that this tale actually reinforces one myth of leadership – the leader as hero who saves the day and without whom everyone else is helpless. I am grateful for that accurate observation. One true anecdote (yes, it's a true story, as all these tales are: Tilly received a Marine Society award in 2006) doesn't always encapsulate as many myth-breaking lessons as we would like. Having a young girl as the prime mover at the heart of this story, and parents who were ready to temporarily cede their own leadership authority to the child based on trusting her judgement and knowledge, helps to break one powerful archetype – the patrician, Churchillian, leader that so many CEOs and other managers model themselves on, often subconsciously. It also makes the point that we must encourage leaders to emerge from unexpected places and recognize them when they do; that in flexible organizations, different people will lead at different times, depending on needs, knowledge, circumstance and particular skills.

4. The 60 Second Leader and…

CONNECTION

Leadership is personal. Mass personalization. And Death came third.

> 'Only connect.'
> E. M. Forster

LEADERSHIP IS PERSONAL

The economist, journalist and author Will Hutton has a story about **Bill Clinton**. Hutton was at a reception with hundreds of others when Clinton swept in with his entourage. He worked the room, shaking hands. When he got to Hutton he paused. 'Will Hutton, right?' said Clinton with a twinkle in his eye. 'I really enjoyed your book,' he said, then shook hands with real warmth, and mentioned both the book title and a point that he remembered from it. Then he was gone, glad-handing the rest of the crowd. Hutton says he was stunned at the level of personal connection achieved in just a few seconds. [1]

Clinton could intimately touch the person he was communicating with (stop snickering: you know what I mean). Reagan could do it too.

MASS PERSONALIZATION

The odd thing is that they could both do it even through television, an impersonal medium, addressing a mass, unseen audience. They were able to keep it personal even though the connection was one-to-many rather than one-to-one.

The ability to connect didn't always work, however. **Colin Powell** tells a cringe-making story about the first meeting between Reagan and Gorbachev in the White House, to discuss nuclear disarmament. Gorbachev showed a complete command of the facts and the arguments, says Powell. Reagan, who had said nothing, then told a folksy story about the difference between Russian and American taxi drivers. It was met with stunned silence. Powell says the whole of the next meeting was spent recovering credibility. [2]

> *'Your job is to touch everyone and get into their soul. Every moment you are in your office, you are useless.'*
> Jack Welch

Rapport is the one-to-one ability to connect. It comes from a genuine interest in others. **Natural projection** is the ability to get past the artificiality of standing on a stage or talking into a TV camera and still connect on a personal level. **Daniel Goleman** says the ability to connect with people one-to-one or one-to-many requires **emotional resonance** – empathy – and says it is the prime requirement of leaders today. Hence his phrase *'primal leadership'.* [3]

You don't have to be the official leader in a group to be the primal leader. Sometimes in a team or even a large organization the official leader may have trouble connecting on a personal level. People then transfer their need for emotional leadership – for a person or value system that helps give meaning to their personal contribution – to someone else they trust and respect, perhaps a deputy or a peer. The formal leader, if they have any sense, then works through that person and ideally learns from them about how to build relationships more effectively. Or the formal leader sees the emotional leader as a threat and sabotages them. Then you are in a real mess.

AND, FINALLY … DEATH CAME THIRD

In a *New York Times* survey, people were asked what they feared most. Death came third. Walking into a crowded room came second. Public speaking came first. [4] Most managers worry about their ability to stand up and move a crowd – but you don't have to be a natural public speaker to connect and communicate effectively. Richard Branson froze and jumped off the stage the first time he was called to give a big speech. Jack Welch stammers. Branson occasionally does, too. Marcus Buckingham, a great orator, used to stammer, too, and says he still feels so sick he almost throws up before going on stage. It doesn't matter if you are not slick. It only matters that you are authentic: people want to hear from the real you. Leadership is personal.

USEFUL CONCEPT

Network leadership: Goleman says the most effective leaders 'are more connected to people *and to networks*' (*author's note*: my emphasis). [5] You can't dominate a network with old-style leadership, but you can emerge, with the network's consent, as one of its leaders, regardless of your formal position or job title. Network connectors who bring talented people together in a community of interest are among the most effective leaders today.

SOURCES AND FURTHER READING

(1) I heard this story from Will Hutton's friend, Richard Reeves.

(2) *My American Journey*, Colin Powell.

(3) *Primal Leadership*, Daniel Goleman, Richard Boyatzis, Annie McKee.

   UK readers note: inexplicably, given the power of that title, this book was renamed *The New Leaders* for publication in the UK.

(4) *And Death Came Third*, Andy Lopata, Peter Roper.

(5) *Primal Leadership* (see note 3).

A 60 Second Leader Tale: Ikea's ten-minute leader

The world's second, third or fourth richest man, depending on how you calculate these things (he disputes that he is any of those, by the way) is **Ingvar Kamprad**. By some calculations, he knocked Bill Gates off the top spot a while back. The founder of *Ikea* leads ... *thriftily* is probably the best way to put it.

What interests me about this is how Kamprad's legendary thrift ends up writ large, multiplied a millionfold, mirrored in the behaviour of thousands of employees, to become the central tenet of *Ikea*'s low-cost culture. Stories about Kamprad's unwillingness to spend money circulate endlessly within *Ikea*, showing (a) the power of leading by example, and (b) the importance of company stories in creating a culture.

These five 10-second Kamprad stories are from Elen Lewis's great little book, *Ikea, A Brand For All The People,* and the sixth is from **Richard Branson**:

---

1. THE RE-USABLE RIBBON

Kamprad was invited to Almhult, the tiny town in Smaland where the first *Ikea* store opened in 1953. A statue of Kamprad in the town centre had been erected and Kamprad was supposed to attend to cut the ribbon and officially inaugurate his statue. When the moment came, instead of cutting the ribbon, Kamprad carefully untied it, rolled it up in his hand and handed it back to the mayor, saying: 'Now you can use this ribbon again.'

2. WHEN THE BOSS SLEPT IN THE CAR

An ex-employee recalls a business trip to a factory in Poland. They were travelling in three cars, but got lost and couldn't find a cheap hotel. The only hotel free in the area was a Marriott, an expensive chain that Kamprad immediately vetoed as it cost too much. They all slept in their cars that night.

3. IS IT CHEAP ENOUGH?

There's the story within *Ikea* of Kamprad, on a store visit, questioning customers as they queue for the checkout. Seizing items from their trolley and basket he keeps asking them how much they paid for their things. Apparently everyone just thought he was a bit crazy. They didn't realize they were being questioned by the *Ikea* founder. Then he would ask them, 'Well, is it worth it? Is this item worth the amount you're paying for it?'

4. BE THE CUSTOMER

Kamprad is famous for playing a game during his arduous 15-hour visits in *Ikea* stores. He pretends that he is a customer shopping with his wife, Margaretha. Kamprad plays both parts. So, during these inspections, he'll walk around pretending his wife is with him, talking to her, asking her opinion. At every room set and display he checks the imaginary shoppers have everything they need. He will say things like: 'So, Margaretha, what do you think of those sofas and where is the pen where we could write down notes about it?' It's as if he's fine-tuning a violin.

5. WHEN THE BOSS HID IN A CARPET

Established sectoral players often gang up on a challenger brand that breaks their conventions and presents itself as the customers' champion. *Ikea*'s prices were so low that the *National Association of Furniture Dealers* in Sweden sent an ultimatum to some suppliers threatening to stop buying from them if they continued to sell to *Ikea*. Both *Ikea* and Kamprad personally were banned from trade shows. Kamprad smuggled himself into one, hiding in a rolled up carpet in the back of a Volvo.

6. THE TEN-MINUTE LEADER

Richard Branson, similarly a leader of challenger brands that like to break sectoral rules, says that Kamprad divides his day into ten-minute sections and is intent on getting the most out of each ten minutes because 'you will never get them back'. So the thrifty leader is even thrifty with his time.

Sources: *Great Ikea, a Brand For All The People*, Elen Lewis (Tales 1–5); *Losing My Virginity*, the autobiography of Richard Branson (Tale 6).

5. The 60 Second Leader and ...

LUCK

The gorilla and the basketball. Can you make your own luck?

> *'I spent 26 years leading expeditions that looked for a lost city under the desert – I wasn't out there for the whole 26 years, I just repeatedly went back to try and find it. It was found by sheer good luck. It turned out it was under the base camp I had been using for the previous 26 years to launch expeditions to find it ...'*
> Sir Ranulph Fiennes, explorer

In an experiment, subjects were asked to watch a video clip of two teams passing a basketball between them, and told they had to count the number of passes. Halfway through the clip, a man dressed in a gorilla suit walked on in the background, beat his chest, then walked off again. Eighty per cent of the subjects failed to spot the gorilla. [1]

If you think success looks like all the things that used to make your company successful, but the fast-changing markets out there constantly re-define what success actually looks like, then you will be unlucky. You will be looking for basketballs and missing gorillas.

> *'But is he lucky?'*
> Napoleon's criterion for appointing a general
> (Apparently this is an apocryphal saying. Shame. I always liked it.)

Luck has become more important to success in recent years, as markets have become less predictable. For example, product life cycles have accelerated, so you are having to bet more often during your career on whether a new product will succeed. Non-commercial organizations are equally under pressure from regulators to change drastically to become less bureaucratic and more customer-focussed. Taking decisions in an age of more variables, more uncertainty, obviously increases the risk of getting it wrong. So, can you make your own luck to increase the odds of getting it right more often?

MAKE YOUR OWN LUCK

Luck is generally seen as an external factor, over which you have no control, but there are also those who claim to be born lucky. Somewhere in between these two extremes hovers the truth about luck: that you can, but only to some extent, make your own.

There is an obvious, but not reliable, correlation between hard work and luck, as the oil magnate John Paul Getty noted:

> *My formula for success is*
> *Rise early.*
> *Work late.*
> *Strike oil.*
> J. P. Getty

OK, he meant it as a tongue-in-cheek comment on the high-risk oil prospecting sector he worked in, but there is also an underlying truth to leadership in this quote: the harder you work and the more opportunities you open up, the luckier you are likely to become. Or, as golfer Gary Player said on being told he had a reputation for being lucky, 'It's funny how the more I practise, the luckier I get.'

The most interesting recent work on luck and organizations was conducted by psychologist Richard Wiseman, [1, 2] whose research seems to find there are two aspects to being lucky. The first is being in the right place at the right time. This serendipity may be largely outside your control, though Tom Peters points out that the more you network outside your conventional circle ('Go to lunch with a freak!' he is fond of shouting), the more chances of encountering opportunity you create for yourself. [3]

Serendipity – stumbling across something useful – is, however, useless without the second aspect of luck, which is recognizing the opportunity. Luck comes to a prepared mind. Most of us aren't awake to unexpected opportunity, says Wiseman, citing the gorilla experiment as evidence. Wiseman identifies four factors in creating your own luck.

- Maximize opportunities. (Be open. Expect the unexpected.)
- Listen to your intuition. We are good at detecting patterns (see Chapter 2, *Intuition*, for more on this).
- Be positive.
- Put bad experiences into perspective.

You can tell from the last two points that, as with others who write on the subject, Wiseman's work veers towards positive thinking and self-help. But, he insists that lucky thinking patterns create real-world business impact. Wiseman experimented with trying to make an organization more lucky by instilling in managers and employees what he says are the positive thought patterns of lucky people. The business claimed to improve its profits by 20 per cent.

USEFUL DISTINCTION

Luck and chance: Leaders have no control over chance, but you may have some control over how lucky you and your organization are.

SOURCES AND FURTHER READING

(1) *Did You Spot The Gorilla? How to recognize hidden opportunities in your life*, Richard Wiseman.

(2) *The Luck Factor: The scientific study of the lucky mind*, Richard Wiseman.

(3) *The Pursuit of Luck*, a list of 50 actions you can take to increase your luck, appeared first in Tom Peters' book *Liberation Management* and can now also be found if you search for it on his website at *www. tompeters.com.*

A 60 Second Leader Tale: Covey on turning janitors into leaders

A manager asked me how to get a team of janitors working in a way where they took responsibility instead of ducking it.

I asked who managed the supplies, cleaning schedules, keeping within budget and so on. He managed all of that. So, my advice was to cede it all step by step to the janitors. Let them set the schedules. Show them how to do the budgeting. The principle at work here is: 'Lead people, manage things.'

He felt this was not possible with manual labour. But, much of what we have to do today is turning manual workers into knowledge workers.*

The janitors now do the planning and doing. The supervisor serves them. He has become a 'servant leader'. Costs are down, incidentally …

Source: My notes from a talk given by **Stephen Covey**.

Before you can lead others you need to be able to take charge of and lead yourself. Frontline leadership, where there is no direct supervision of others in a hierarchy, often consists of this initiative-taking self-leadership, and leading peers by example.

---

* The phrase 'knowledge worker' is commonly taken to mean what white-collar workers have to evolve into. That's wrong. Manual workers are becoming knowledge workers too.

6. The 60 Second Leader and …

OPTIMISM

Confronting reality. The one and the many. Lead or led.
Faith and fate.

> *'The optimists. Oh, they were the ones who said, "We're going to be out by*
> *Christmas."And Christmas would come, and Christmas would go. Then*
> *they'd say, "We're going to be out by Easter."And Easter would come, and*
> *Easter would go. And then Thanksgiving, and then it would be Christmas*
> *again. And they died of a broken heart. This is a very important lesson. You*
> *must never confuse faith that you will prevail in the end – which you can never*
> *afford to lose – with the discipline to confront the most brutal facts of your*
> *current reality, whatever they might be.'*
> Admiral Jim Stockdale, talking to Jim Collins about his time in the no-
> torious 'Hanoi Hilton' prisoner-of-war camp in Vietnam. The optimists,
> said the Admiral, died first. [1]

CONFRONTING REALITY

We are told there is too much optimism in business; that leaders talk up
themselves and their organizations and fail to confront reality when it
threatens their upbeat view of their own performance. [2] I think that is
absolutely right. But, we also know that the mood of a leader is infectious
and can spread like wildfire. For most of us, most of the time, work isn't the
equivalent of a prisoner-of-war camp. I'm not sure Jim Collins' use of Admi-
ral Stockdale as an extreme example is always helpful, as it is hard to inspire
people around a position of stoicism. So how do you maintain a positive,
can-do spirit in your organization without ignoring uncomfortable facts?

Antonio Gramsci, the Italian political theorist, largely solved the problem
for us in the early twentieth century. He doesn't start off too encouragingly:

'Turn your face violently towards things as they exist now. Not as you'd like them to be, not as you think they were ten years ago, not as they're written about in sacred texts, but as they really are: the contradictory, stony ground of the present ...' he wrote. Ouch. Try inspiring people with that and see if they walk into work with a spring in their step.

But, then Gramsci comes up with a formulation that almost reconciles the problem. Become, he says, and show others how to become 'a pessimist of the intellect and an optimist of the will.' Maybe tweaking Gramsci's phrase to become a 'sceptic of the intellect and an optimist of the will' tips the balance in favour of realistic optimism, rather than still leaving us with that negative word 'pessimist' in the mix.

THE ONE AND THE MANY

Leaders are at their most effective when they are most in touch with reality, and this happens when they are almost viscerally in synch with the people and markets they lead and serve. Synchronicity is a better word than alignment to describe this ideal state. Organizational effectiveness gurus like to tell us everyone and everything work best when aligned. But people, markets, culture, emergent trends ... none of these things are linear, nor are they static, nor can they be placed alongside each other. In the real world, they mesh, overlap and interact. They need to synchronize rather than align.

The relationship between the one and the many is at the heart of leadership. Lord Byron put it this way: 'And when we think we lead, we are most led.' This may at first glance appear like that old saw, 'Quickly, I must hurry, for there go my people and I am their leader.' But it's not about populism or tails wagging dogs. It's about tapping into and being part of the *zeitgeist*, being synchronized or in tune with the state of things.

An analogy would be what long-distance runners call being 'in the zone.' It's about being able to 'wick up' reality (see Chapter 3, *Decisions*) and being able to lead accordingly. It's about leaders being part of things, not an

external change agent acting on them. It's the spasm in George Soros' back that tells him a market correction is coming.

FAITH AND FATE

There is a powerful insight from the Scottish mountaineer W. H. Murray which is usually quoted to show how commitment can put fate on your side – how faith can invoke fate, if you like. It's quoted below.

Murray seems to be talking about bending the universe to your will, but what he is actually observing is that, if you are in tune with what is emerging, you can be a powerful accelerant for change. There is an interplay between great leadership, events, trends, the organization, the people in it and the market 'out there' that goes far beyond one person exercising their will over others. Murray captures that symbiosis here, even if he appears to misinterpret it as the triumph of individual will, just as he misquotes Goethe:

'Concerning all acts of initiative (and creation) there is one elementary truth, the ignorance of which kills countless ideas and splendid plans: that the moment one definitely commits oneself, then Providence moves too.

'All sorts of things occur to help one that would never otherwise have occurred. A whole stream of events issues from the decision, raising in one's favour all manner of unforeseen incidents and meetings and material assistance which no man could have dreamt would have come his way.

'I have learned a deep respect for one of Goethe's couplets:

'Whatever you can do, or dream you can, begin it.
Boldness has genius, power and magic in it.' [3]

SOURCES AND FURTHER READING

(1) *Good to Great*, Jim Collins. Collins calls the ability to confront the brutal truth and still retain belief that you will prevail *The Stockdale Paradox*.

(2) *Confronting Reality*, Larry Bossidy and Ram Charan.

(3) Goethe scholars have failed to find these words or their German equivalent in any of Goethe's work. It doesn't diminish their power, though. The strongest argument against Murray is the usual one: 'Where's the control group?' i.e. all those people who committed themselves and went down in a blaze of unsung glory because Providence didn't move. It only works if your decision is in synch with what is unformed yet ready to emerge. Surfers do not create the waves they surf.

A 60 Second Leader Tale: Why your mood is so important

> *'A leader's mood is infectious. It can spread like wildfire through an organiza-tion. You can poison or uplift the mood without realizing it.'*
> Mike Harris, founding CEO, *First Direct Bank*

Be very aware of how your slightest signals can affect people when you are in a position of power (that's for all you formal leaders) or people look to you for a lead (informal leaders).

'No one wants to work for a grouch. Research has proven it: optimistic, enthusiastic leaders more easily retain their people compared with those bosses who tend towards negative moods.

Numerous studies show that when the leader is in a happy mood, the people around him view everything in a more positive light. That, in turn, makes them more optimistic about achieving their goals, enhances their creativity and the efficiency of their decision-making, and predisposes them to be helpful.'

In more than one sense, then, leadership is truly viral.

Source: *Primal Leadership*, Daniel Goleman, Richard Boyatzis and Annie McKee.

LEADING THE ORGANIZATION

7. The 60 Second Leader and ...

STRATEGY

The one thing you need to know about strategy ... and horses.

'We have a "strategic plan". It's called "doing things".'
Herb Kelleher, *Southwest Airlines*

THE ONE THING YOU NEED TO KNOW

Strategy and *execution* are not mutually exclusive and they are not sequential. There isn't the neat linear division between the two that most management schools like to teach. This is what Henry Mintzberg gets and other strategists don't. [1] Mintzberg's insight says strategy doesn't necessarily come first – 'think' then 'do'. Strategy and execution intertwine, so stop separating them in your head.

'Virtually everything that has been written about strategy-making depicts it as a deliberate process. First we think, then we act. We formulate, then we implement. The progression seems so perfectly sensible. Why would anybody want to proceed differently?' he writes. [1]

He goes on: 'Everyone knows where a straight line goes ... but a squiggly line can go anywhere. Computers generate straight lines. Life generates squiggly ones. That's why your predictable business strategies never turn out the way you expect ... Smart strategists appreciate that they cannot always be smart enough to think through everything in advance.'

Why do so few other strategists get this? Breaking the distinction between strategy and execution frees leaders at all levels of the organization to be more agile.

BUT DON'T THEN MAKE THE MISTAKE ...

... of confusing strategy with operational effectiveness. '*To be the best*' is not a strategy. 'You need to be clear on the difference between **operational effectiveness** and **strategy**,' Michael Porter, [2] often dubbed the *King of Strategy*, told me in an interview. 'Operational effectiveness means being better than the competition at deploying "best practices". In other words, you are saying: "We are the same but better". This is just running the same race and betting you can run it faster than the competition. Strategic positioning, by contrast, means choosing which race to run. It involves creating a unique and sustainable position.'

STRATEGY IS NOT A HAMMER

Formal leaders can get locked into following company strategy blindly and, when it isn't working, resort to *Dobin's Law.* 'When in doubt, use a bigger hammer'. To a person who has a hammer, everything starts to look like a nail. In other words, an inflexible strategy can programme your organization's actions and responses in ways that are too rigid and often inappropriate.

Which is why Mintzberg says: 'Strategies are to organizations what blinkers are to horses.' Note this isn't always a bad thing, as blinkers keep the horse focussed on running its race rather than veering off at a tangent. But it does mean you can miss alternatives or fail to notice when changes in the market are making your strategy redundant.

TALKING OF HORSES ...

Here's a reminder from Gary Hamel [3] that part of the role of leaders at all levels is to look out for signs that your strategy needs renewing:

> '*Dakota tribal wisdom says that when you discover you're on a dead horse, the best strategy is to dismount. Of course, there are other strategies. You can change riders. You can get a committee to study the dead horse. You can benchmark how other companies ride dead horses. You can declare that it is cheaper to feed a dead horse. You can harness several dead horses together. But after*

you've tried all these things, you're still going to have to dismount. The tempta-
tion to stay on a dead horse can be overwhelming, but working ever harder to
improve the efficiency of a worn-out strategy is ultimately futile. Strategy decay
is not something that might happen; it's something that is happening.'

USEFUL CONCEPT

System Dynamics: Developed at the Massachusetts Institute of Technology. Models
the strategies of your organization and other players in your sector to help you anticipate and avoid strategy decay.

SOURCES AND FURTHER READING

(1) *Strategy Bites Back*, Henry Mintzberg.

(2) Michael Porter's seminal book *Competitive Strategy* presents his early
work on the structure of industries and the choice of position within
them. *Competitive Advantage* further developed his work on strategic
positioning.

(3) *Leading The Revolution*, by Gary Hamel.

A 60 Second Leader Tale: Leadership is allowing ordinary people to be extraordinary

Leadership is not a war for talent. It's about allowing ordinary people to deliver extraordinary performances consistently. General Colin Powell, former Secretary of State, offers an example:

'We were trying to figure out how much practice ammunition a tank crew had to fire to become proficient. One thing we knew was that Soviet crews fired about one-tenth as many rounds in training as American crews did. The cost differential was tremendous. Every time we fired from a tank, it cost the taxpayer from $200 to $1,000, depending on the type of round. And each of our crews fired approximately one hundred rounds a year.

The Army's training technicians had designed simulators and devices like video games that would allow our crews to become proficient using less live ammo. We wanted to find out what combination of actual firing and use of training devices produced the best performance.

One tank battalion was given the maximum number of rounds. Another got fewer rounds. Another got fewer rounds still and more time on the simulator-trainers. The acid test was to take these differently prepared battalions out to the major qualification range, give them the same number of rounds and see which did best.

The answer turned out to be "none of the above." The battalions that did best were those with the best commanders. A good commander could motivate his men to excel under any conditions. "We're gonna win even if they give us one lousy round," was the winning attitude.

The new technologies were adopted, and they did make a difference. But we never lost sight of the reality that people, particularly gifted commanders, are what makes units successful. The way I like to put it, leadership is the art of accomplishing more than the science of management says is possible.'

Source: *My American Journey*, General Colin Powell.

8. The 60 Second Leader and ...

COMPETITION

Refuse to compete. The blue and the red. Protect your advantage.

> 'We still use these old warfare metaphors for business leadership, quoting ancient Chinese generals and applying them to business. But "beat the enemy" doesn't work. You need to compete to be unique, not the best.'
> Professor Michael Porter, in an interview with the author [1]

BLUE OCEAN STRATEGY

All the big strategy thinkers have been singing the same song for the past five years or more. From **Gary Hamel** and **C. K. Prahalad** [2] to **Michael Porter**, from **Renee Mauborgne** to **Kjell Nordstrom**, the mantra is: 'Don't compete. Be unique.' Ironic, really, that they are all competitors in terms of their book sales, the business schools they represent, and on the lecture circuit, but all are putting the same argument forward. In other words, they are doing what they tell us not to do. Or it could just be that if they all agree on this, they are all right.

Renee Mauborgne and W. Chan Kim put it most evocatively with their phrase 'Blue Ocean Strategy'. [3]

THE BLUE AND THE RED

Mauborgne and Kim say that a **blue ocean** is a new or previously unnoticed market space. You create it by identifying a set of unserved customers or spot an unmet need among existing customers. Then you work up a value proposition for them that is different to anything else out there.

The 2006 *Nobel Prize* winner **Muhammad Yunus** is an example of a blue ocean strategist. Lending to the poor and destitute – micro-lending – was a non-existent market sector. The existing banks refused to accept it was a viable market. Yet Yunus grew his **Grameen Bank**, which only lends to the poor, into a profitable £2.5 billion business (multiply that by about 1.8 at current exchange rates to get US dollars).

Most markets in the developed world are a ***red ocean***, where the competition all agree what the market is and all have well-defined often lookalike offers competing against each. In many cases this leads to **strategic convergence** – where you and your competitors all follow the same strategy and end up competing on price.

You need to take the blue pill rather than the red pill (sorry, slipped from oceans to *The Matrix* there) because red markets are saturated, with head-to-head competition forcing down price. Blue ocean strategists stake out their own territory.

At least that's the theory. In practice, the best you can hope for is a temporary monopoly [4] (unless you are Bill Gates, in which case you manage to spin it out for years), since competitors will appear on your patch and start competing with you almost immediately. What was blue will turn red faster than you think.

PROTECTING YOUR ADVANTAGE

Michael Porter and others point out that having a unique value creation chain that is hard to copy, not just a unique or unusual product or service, helps protect your competitive advantage. Where some of the big strategists are weak, though, is in recognizing the value of a unique culture in setting you apart from the competition. I've seen Porter describe at length *Southwest Airlines*' hard-to-copy value chain and how its strategy is based on a unique set of trade-offs and a set of interdependent activities that are 'a good fit', without once mentioning that company's unique people culture. That's strategists for you.

USEFUL CONCEPT

A caveat on 'refuse to compete': 'The word *competition* comes from the Latin and literally means *seeking together* or *choosing to run the same race*. But, in an age of abundance, the tracks are pretty crowded.' – *Kjell Nordstrom and Jonas Ridderstrale.* [4] But the one caveat I would add is that the 'don't compete' rule doesn't apply to operations. However desirable and different your offer is, you have to match the best operational performance, such as delivery times.

AND, FINALLY ... MAINTAIN A BALANCE

I heard Renee Mauborgne make the point recently that you need to balance your portfolio of products and services between current revenue generators – red ocean products and services – and emerging or future products and services – blue ocean strategies.

SOURCES AND FURTHER READING

(1) Professor Michael Porter, in an interview with Phil Dourado.

(2) *The Future of Competition*, Gary Hamel and C. K. Prahalad.

(3) *Blue Ocean Strategy*, Renee Mauborgne and W. Chan Kim.

(4) *Funky Business*, Kjell Nordstrom and Jonas Ridderstrale.

A 60 Second Leader Tale: Muhammad Yunus' Blue Ocean Strategy

I'm not one for the 'great man' school of history, but there are a few obvious Mandela-stature exceptions – and **Muhammad Yunus** is one of them.

Yunus is an economics professor. The major banks laughed at his suggestion that they break destitute Bangladeshis out of the poverty cycle with a new concept that gave them an alternative to loan sharks – micro-lending.

So, he lent a group of villagers the money in his own pocket – the equivalent of £14 or around US$25 – to buy the materials they needed to set up micro-businesses. They all paid him back with interest. His new idea – micro-lending – grew into the £2.5 billion (almost $5 billion at current exchange rates) *Grameen Bank* that is owned by its users, is estimated to have helped hundreds of thousands of people out of poverty … and continues to make a profit.

The false assumption that the rest of the banking industry's practice rested on was that the very poor are a bad credit risk. Yunus' small-scale experiment suggested they were wrong. As he scaled his operations up, it became clear that for the customer group who made up his main constituency – rural women – they were completely wrong. The proportion of *Grameen* borrowers who default on their loan is tiny compared with traditional bank lending.

Yunus then spotted that, with mobile phones, local growers and craftspeople – mostly women – could jump past middlemen, who tended to exploit them with very low prices, to negotiate direct with buyers further away, increasing their bargaining power.

So, he launched *Grameen Phone*, a phone rental scheme with its own network, to get mobile phones into the hands of the poor. Now if you go to Bangladesh '*Grameen Phone*' is likely to pop up on your phone screen as your local provider. It has become, like the bank, a highly profitable success story.

Yunus still lives in a tiny apartment in Bangladesh. He explained once that he developed the idea for the Grameen Bank during the Bangladesh famine in the 1970s. He had become increasingly disillusioned that people were dying while he and other economics professors were sitting around in Chittagong University teaching elegant economic theories 'whereas in fact the starvation all around us showed we knew nothing. What we were teaching wasn't helping.'

He once said to *The Guardian* newspaper: 'One day we will look in museums and say to our children, "That's what poverty looked like."'

That sounds naïve – until you look at what he has achieved so far. Fifty other countries – including the US – have taken up micro-lending. Yunus' work helped prompt **C. K. Prahalad's** book *The Fortune At The Bottom Of The Pyramid*, which looks at extending capitalist practice to embrace the world's poorest with Grameen-style offerings that make healthy profits while at the same time helping people out of poverty.

Now, like I said, I am wary of the whole 'great man as leader' or 'great man as forger of history' school of thinking (it's nearly always men). But every now and again, someone comes along that makes us see the world afresh and inspires us by showing us we can do the apparently undoable and take the lead to make major change happen. Sounds like a leader to me.

9. The 60 Second Leader and …

ACTION

To do or to be. A decision is not action. The six obstacles to action.

> *'Leadership, like swimming, cannot be learned by reading about it.'*
> Henry Mintzberg, reminding us that leaders need to learn by doing

TO *DO* OR TO *BE*: THAT IS THE QUESTION

Hamlet got it wrong. John Boyd got it right.

Boyd is the creator of the *OODA loop* fast decision matrix (see Chapter 3, *Decisions*). I thought OODA loop was one of Willy Wonka's midgets, but my son says that's an Oompa Loompa. What a difference a couple of letters make.

Boyd's insight was that people become leaders for one of two reasons: either to *do* something or to *be* somebody. [1] We all know too many bosses who became 'leaders' to *be* somebody. Boyd defined them as people who give up some of their integrity to achieve advancement in an organization. Hence the paradox that often the best leaders are not in a formal leadership position in the hierarchy, because they refuse to choose placement over integrity.

Boyd said it's the fundamental choice facing us all in life: to *do* or to *be*. There's a lot of truth in that. Positional leaders – those who are most driven by the need to *be* in a leadership position – often have a stifling effect on growth, as they see other potential and existing leaders as threats.

WHAT DON'T YOU DO?

A good drummer will tell you it's knowing when not to hit a drum that marks out good drummers from the average; the silent spaces between the action are in fact part of the action. Similarly, a good leader knows that a *To Don't* list is as important for success as a *To Do* list. What you don't do defines you as much as what you do.

American sociologist Jamie L. Mullaney has analyzed this in a book called *Everyone Is Not Doing It: Abstinence and Personal Identity*. Laurie Taylor, the UK sociologist, puts it this way: 'For many people, abstaining labels like vegan, virgin or non-smoker are proud declarations of who they are. In a world stuffed with choices and options, not doing something may be a highly significant move.'

Rene Carayol, [2] a British leadership guru whom I have a lot of time for, says it is all about where you make your stand; that the best leaders make it clear what they stand for and constantly reinforce that with what they do and what they choose not to do.

Action has the power to shift the thought patterns of yourself and others. We don't think ourselves into a new way of acting: we act ourselves into a new way of thinking.

Of course, the opposite is also true. There are those for whom 'not doing' becomes a frozen strategy in itself. 'Wait and see' leaders who procrastinate – on the assumption that if you don't make a decision you can't be blamed if it's wrong, or that things will sort themselves out – turn inaction from a choice into a habit. Don't forget reason Number 4 of Dotlich and Cairo's 11 main reasons leaders fail: procrastination. [3]

A DECISION IS NOT ACTION

But, equally, don't mistake meetings and decisions for action. I once worked with a senior figure in Prime Minister Tony Blair's inner circle. She told me that his first few weeks in the job were frustrating ones for the new PM. He made decisions, then couldn't understand why they hadn't been actioned. The levers of power didn't seem to be connected to anything.

There's perhaps a twofold conceit lurking here that many leaders are guilty of. First is the 'make it so' conceit – the phrase used by Jean Luc Picard,

Captain of the second *Starship Enterprise*. Just because you tell people to do things doesn't mean they have the resources, time, structure, systems, their own levers of power and the will to 'make it so'. The second layer of conceit is assuming that where leaders hold their meetings and make decisions is where the action is. If the leaders are at the centre of the organization, whereas the action actually takes place at the edges of most organizations, there will be a constant reality problem. Stanford Professor Bob Sutton says leaders need to learn to 'use plans, analysis, meetings and presentations to inspire deeds, not as a substitute for action.' [4]

USEFUL CONCEPT

The Six Obstacles to Action: 1. Knowing what to do is not enough. 2. Talk substitutes for action. 3. Memory substitutes for thinking. 4. Fear prevents acting on knowledge. 5. Measurement obstructs good judgement. 6. Internal competition turns allies into enemies. [4]

SOURCES AND FURTHER READING

(1)   *Boyd: The fighter pilot who changed the art of war*, Robert Coram.

(2)   *www.carayol.com*.

(3)   *Why CEOs Fail*, David Dotlich, Peter Cairo *et al.*

(4)   *The Knowing–Doing Gap*, Jeffrey Pfeffer and Bob Sutton.

A 60 Second Leader Tale: Ricardo Semler on why your recruitment doesn't work

Ricardo Semler leads in possibly the most radical place to work in the world – the group of companies that make up Brazil's *Semco SA*. Everything is constantly questioned at *Semco*; nothing is taken for granted. Which is how they came up with a radically different way of recruiting, which keeps their employee turnover at 1–2 per cent per annum. Semler explains in this 60 Second Leader Tale:

GET THE RIGHT PEOPLE

'A key part of leadership is getting the right people. But recruitment today is like internet dating. Two dates and you get married forever? That's why your employee turnover is so high and you are so often disappointed by some of the people you recruit.'

How *Semco* recruits leaders

Step 1

'At *Semco* we recruit leaders differently. We employ 4,000 people. When a business unit comes up with something new, first of all we ask people in-house "Do you need a leader for this new thing you are doing?" Usually they say yes.'

The internal discount

'Then we ask "Is one of you right to be this leader?" We discount internal people 30 per cent when applying for a new role, when we are scoring them against the profile. Because the 30 per cent is the existing value of knowing we can work with them and they with us.'

The recruitment ad

'When we place an ad. for a position it says something like: "Interested in working for us? We want to see if we like you and vice versa."'

The recruitment conversation

'We then have a long conversation with all the candidates. Anyone interested in the new appointment – internal candidates, the people they will be working with, external candidates – joins the conversation. We invite some of the candidates back to have lunch with us, maybe five or six times. Then we all get together to make the decision – including the people they will work with. It takes longer than how other companies recruit. That's why our turnover is between 1 and 2 percent.'

It's not about talent

Semco's way of working, says Semler, liberates ordinary people to achieve extraordinary things for the company: 'You don't want too much talent. You want a cut of humanity.'

The best recruitment takes the decision out of the hands of the top bosses

'We recently had a cocktail party to celebrate the ten-year anniversary since I last made a decision.'

Source: My notes from talking with Ricardo Semler in London, asking him questions by email (which he kindly answered while riding his exercise bike first thing in the morning – that's when he handles his email) and then hearing him talk at *Leaders in London 2006.*

Author's note: Even if you don't go as far as Semler, **Jim Clemmer** reports that 'a study by the *Center for Creative Leadership* found that when one individual made hiring decisions for management positions, the newly hired manager was judged to be successful just 35 per cent of the time. When a hiring team of four or five made the decision, success rose to 55 per cent. But when the small group included both customers and subordinates, success rates soared to 70 per cent.' From Jim's book *The Leader's Digest.*

10. The 60 Second Leader and …

EXECUTION

The great un-idea. The language of action. Three core processes.

The sculptor Auguste Rodin was once asked: 'How do you make your marble horses so lifelike?' Irritated by the questioner, Rodin supposedly replied:

'Take a large piece of marble.
Take a hammer and a chisel.
Cut away everything that doesn't look like a horse.'

A lot of 'visionary' business leadership seems like Rodin's advice – holding out the promise of an answer, but empty when it comes to execution. Recent books such as **Larry Bossidy** and **Ram Charan**'s *Execution* have switched the emphasis. There is a growing awareness that true leaders get their hands dirty rather than proclaiming the vision and strategy from on high and keeping themselves distant from the action.

THE GREAT 'UN-IDEA'

Execution was voted the number one business issue facing readers of *Strategy + Business* magazine at the end of 2005. It received 49 per cent of the votes. Commenting on its importance, **Rosabeth Moss Kanter** wrote, 'Execution is the *un-idea* … rather than chasing new management fad(s) or expecting still another magic bullet to come along, companies should focus on execution to effectively use the organizational tools we already have.' [1]

Bossidy and Charan's books [2] help remind us that execution is not tactical. It's a discipline at the heart of leadership. It has to be built into your strategy, and embedded in your company architecture.

THE LANGUAGE OF ACTION

Active language is the tool leaders use to get things done, argue Bossidy and Charan, in particular *robust dialogue,* as they call it. Speaking the plain truth embeds your culture in reality, which becomes the cornerstone of execution. Rather than deferring to power, or playing power games between departments, corporate conversations made up of *robust dialogue* encourage a culture of getting things done. The effect is to 'bring reality to the surface through openness, candour and informality.'

Bossidy and Charan stress that *robust dialogue* ends with 'closure' – committing to an outcome with clear accountability and deadlines that people stick to. You can see what Rosabeth Moss Kanter meant by execution being the ultimate 'un-idea'.

GOOD COMPANIES YELL AT EACH OTHER

I heard Bossidy explaining the need for robust dialogue recently in an on-stage interview. Here's what he said:

'You have to let people argue with you ... Good companies yell at each other. Too many places don't have that. I don't mean arguing for personal reasons. I mean passionately arguing the right things to do. For too many people, when they become a leader, self-exaltation takes place. They don't want to hear any criticism of their views ... That's when good ideas get stifled and people stop putting them forward.' [3]

According to Bossidy and Charan, the leader's seven essential behaviours that contribute to a culture of execution are:

1 Know your people and your business.
2 Insist on realism.
3 Set real goals and priorities.

4   Follow through.

5   Reward doers.

6   Expand people's capabilities.

7   Know yourself.

THREE CORE PROCESSES OF EXECUTION

People, strategy and operations processes should not be seen as separate entities, argue Bossidy and Charan. It is by bringing them together that you build the discipline of execution into an organization.

USEFUL CONCEPT

Leadership as design: *Ron Crossland* at *Bluepoint Leadership* [4] rightly points out that execution without a systems view is simply a modern version of faster-better-cheaper, which will run you headlong into the law of diminishing returns. With great insight, Ron points out that 'the source leadership dimension behind this action bias, I believe, is *the leader as architect* ... The right architecture can yield execution. But execution alone rarely produces the right architecture.' I would add my own observation here that business architecting isn't a godlike, top-down process. It needs to allow middle-level managers and frontline people to share in leading by designing their own work processes.

SOURCES AND FURTHER READING

(1) *Strategy + Business* magazine, December 2005 *www.strategy-business. com.*

(2) *Confronting Reality* and *Execution*, Larry Bossidy and Ram Charan.

(3) Larry Bossidy, former CEO of *Honeywell* and former Chairman of *GE*, speaking with Tom Peters at the *North American Conference on Customer Management*, Orlando, Florida, October 2005.

(4) *www.bluepointleadership.com.* I recommend Ron's e-newsletter *The Point.*

A *60 Second Leader Tale: Collins, Roddick, red flags and red letters*

What 'red flag' mechanisms do you have in place to allow others to challenge your formal leaders and the CEO, with the guarantee that those formal leaders will give the matter their absolute attention?

Jim Collins coined the phrase *red flag mechanisms* to refer to voluntary self-limitations that formal leaders build into a traditional structure to allow people to be heard.

JIM COLLINS' RED FLAGS

Red flag mechanisms are the equivalent of permission to stop the production line given to factory floor employees if they spot a quality problem. Collins gives each of his students permission to 'red flag' and stop his lectures with any point they want to make, once a semester.

Collins says he got the idea from a friend of his who introduced a practice he calls 'short pay'. He has an agreement with his customers that if his company lets them down in any way, the customer can 'short pay' that month without giving any warning: instead of paying the amount due, they hold back an amount (the customer decides how much). It acts as a red flag to action, says his friend.

ANITA RODDICK'S RED LETTERS

Body Shop founders Anita and Gordon Roddick used to do something similar, I heard Anita Roddick explain once. They handed out ten red envelopes to each employee. If an employee had a concern about how the company was run, they could put it in a red envelope and submit it to the Board. The Board had to make decisions about the points raised in the red letters as the first item on the agenda.

Red flag mechanisms are a way of building challenge and even sometimes defiance into a structure; of redressing power imbalances that are built into hierarchies; of allowing people to be heard.

Such mechanisms need to have built into them the condition that there is no disciplinary comeback. Collins recounts how one student used her red flag to stop his lecture one day and berate him for not running the lecture very well.

BONES' 'GET OUT OF JAIL FREE' CARD

These *60 Second Leader Tales* are all true stories, but I can't resist illustrating this one with a piece of dialogue between two characters in an episode of the TV drama series *Bones,* because it offers a neat twist on the red flag idea.

Bones, a forensic pathologist, decides she has to quit, reluctantly. She loves her job, but cannot take being told what to do by a new boss. The new boss can see what's coming and wants to find a way they can work together. The conversation goes like this, at a table in a diner:

Bones: We have a problem … I have a problem with control and authority.

New Boss: Can you see a way out of it?

B: No. (Seems to be preparing to offer her resignation)

NB: Look: I'm in charge, but, out of respect for you … do you play Monopoly?

B: (*Frowns, puzzled*). Y-e-s.

NB: Well, in Monopoly they have that thing called a 'Get Out Of Jail Free' card. Like I said, I'm in charge, but out of respect for you, you have permission to defy me. No consequences.

B: How many can I have?

NB: One a week.

B: Five per case.

NB: Three per case.

B: Done.

They shake hands.

Lesson? Hierarchies come with an in-built authority problem. People are increasingly less deferential to authority and need mechanisms to allow them to subvert the hierarchy when it is important to them to get a point across and the power imbalance is preventing it. 'Challenge me when you need to' is a powerful message for a formal leader to issue. 'Defy me when you need to' is an even braver one.

11. The 60 Second Leader and ...

MANAGEMENT

Manager or leader? Which are you expected to be?

This particular question is a dead man walking. It should have been buried and forgotten years ago. But people are slow to let go of ideas. *The essential truth is that management and leadership are different modes, but managers and leaders are the same people.* And, as an important aside, people without 'manager' in their job title are often leaders too.

The 'Can managers lead?' debate was started by a *Harvard Business Review* article written by **Abraham Zaleznik** in 1977. [1] Zaleznik claimed the traits of a good manager were incompatible with leadership. 'Because leaders and managers are basically different, the conditions favourable to one may be inimical to the growth of the other,' he wrote.

MANAGEMENT VERSUS LEADERSHIP
From the thinking of Zaleznik and others came a stream of clichés splitting the world into managers and leaders. It's a dichotomy in which management is always presented as low science and leadership as high art. Even today you find glib phrases such as this tripping off the tongue of management consultants (or should that be leadership consultants?):

- 'Managers do things right, leaders do the right things.'
- 'You manage things, but you lead people.'
- 'Management is climbing the ladder; leadership is making sure it's up against the right wall.'
- 'Managers enforce the rules. Leaders break them.'

LEADERS DO MANAGE

There is, of course, some truth in all these statements – especially the last one. But sound-bite polarizations are like the 'help' button on your PC: invariably less helpful than they seem. The implicit assumption behind the rise of leadership as a separatist movement is that leaders are more highly evolved, and somehow better than managers. It has allowed some 'leaders' to revel in saying they are vision people who 'don't do detail', as if detail is something you can leave to managers and other non-strategic lower life forms. These leaders are fakes. We all know them. Distance from detail is not a badge of leadership: it's a sign of detachment from reality.

YOU NEED TO BE BOTH

Things have evolved since Zaleznik's paper in 1977 and you can no longer get by with the assumption that managers are from Mars and leaders are from Venus. With flatter hierarchies, you need managers at all levels who can act as leaders.

THE REAL DIFFERENCE

When in doubt, defer to John Kotter, who is right most of the time. This isn't pretty, but it rings true: 'Increasingly, those in managerial jobs can be usefully thought of as those who create agendas filled with plans (the management part) and visions (the leadership part), as people who create implementation capacity networks through a well-organized hierarchy (management) and a complex web of aligned relationships (leadership), and who execute through both controls (management) and inspiration (leadership).' [2]

That's unwieldy in its wording, but it's truer than the glib 'either/or' definitions. The great (in my view) Jim Clemmer presents some of the differences graphically in this table from his book *The Leader's Digest*. [3] A typical

manager/leader will probably do all these things and more in the course of a single day. You can see how, if you and your organization want to improve, you will want to shift some of your activities from the left-hand column and start living more in the right-hand column.

Management	Leadership
Commanding	Coaching
Solving problems	Enabling others to solve problems
Directing and controlling	Teaching and engaging
Seeing people as they are	Developing people into what they could be
Empowering	Partnering
Operating	Improving
Pushing	Pulling
Heroic manager	Facilitative leader
Quick fix to symptoms	Search for systemic root causes

USEFUL CONCEPT

What wolves can teach you about leadership: Let different people lead at different times, rather than assume the primacy of one leader. A painting of a pack of wolves in C. K. Prahalad's office symbolizes this. 'With wolves, solidarity is first,' says Prahalad. 'But when they hunt, they change roles. The implicit hierarchy depends on who does what.' [4]

SOURCES AND FURTHER READING

(1) 'Managers and Leaders: Are They Different?' Abraham Zaleznik, *Harvard Business Review* article, 1977.

(2) John Kotter's '10 Observations' from his book *What Leaders Really Do*. See also Kotter's book *A Force for Change: How Leadership Differs from Management*.

(3) *The Leader's Digest*, Jim Clemmer.

(4) C. K. Prahalad talking to Jennifer Reingold, *Fast Company Magazine* article, July 2001.

A 60 Second Leader Tale: Michael Eisner's Gong Show

Michael Eisner is often criticized for his time as head of *Disney*, due to his famous abrasiveness and the reported difficulty he had in sharing power. But I feel one thing he had in common with Walt Disney – whom he is commonly compared unfavourably with by Disney-philes – is his belief in the supremacy of ideas. In this *60 Second Leader Tale* he gives an example of how to lead innovation:

'At *Disney*, we feel the only way to succeed creatively is to fail. A company like ours must create an atmosphere in which people feel safe to fail. This means creating an organization where failure is not only tolerated, but fear of criticism for submitting a foolish idea is abolished. If not, people become too cautious. They hunker down, afraid to speak up, to rock the boat, afraid of being ridiculed.

Potentially brilliant ideas are never uttered, and therefore never heard. Wayne Gretsky, the great ice hockey player, said, "You miss 100 percent of the shots you never take."

Not long after I came to *Disney* a bunch of us would get together with our creative executives for what we called The Gong Show. We would meet and toss ideas around … mostly ideas for television shows and movies. Anyone who wanted could present an idea for a movie or a TV show. Rank had no privileges.

For example, our flagship *Disney Feature Animation*, which had a string of blockbusters, has its own Gong Show three times a year. Anybody who wants to – and I mean anybody – gets a chance to pitch an idea for an animated film to a small group of executives … There are usually about 40 presenters.

For this to work, you have to have an environment where people feel safe about giving their ideas. And while we do not pull our punches when people present their ideas, we create an atmosphere in which each idea can receive full and serious consideration. Yes, we tell people if we think an idea won't work, but we tell them why and we tell them how it might be improved.

If you take the time to listen and to be honest in your reactions, if you create a setting that recognizes that ideas come in all shapes and sizes and are willing to follow the creative mind wherever it goes – something you can never predict – people begin to understand a basic fact: if you have an idea you believe in and can express it, it will be considered …

Several of our better animated features have come out of the Gong Shows and some of our other major winners out of similar kinds of programs in other parts of the company.'

Source: Michael Eisner, then *Disney* supremo, talking in Chicago. Reported in *The Book of Leadership Wisdom: Classic Writings of Legendary Business Leaders*, edited by Peter Krass.

12. The 60 Second Leader and ...

CHANGE

Built to change. Idealistic versus naturalistic change. Epiphanies.

> *'Here is Edward Bear, coming downstairs now, bump, bump, bump, on the back of his head behind Christopher Robin. It is, as far as he knows, the only way of coming downstairs, but sometimes he feels there really is another way, if only he could stop bumping for a moment and think of it.'*
> A. A. Milne, *Winnie the Pooh*

If the rate of change within your organization fails to match the rate of change outside, then you're in trouble. Since the future happens faster than before (as Gary Hamel points out), most organizations find themselves playing permanent catch-up, and in need of **constant renewal**.

The challenge of renewal comes in one of two forms, according to Hamel:

1   how to revitalize a moribund company; and
2   how to preserve vitality in a successful organization. [1]

You may find different parts of your organization present a mix of these two challenges. The task facing leaders is not to manage change – a phrase that is thankfully on the decline – but to create organizations that have change built into them. This is why the old large-change mental model of 'unfreeze, change, re-freeze' is so outdated now. There should never be a frozen state. The organization needs to be *built to change*. The uncomfortable fact for command and control leaders is that for an organization to be self-adjusting you have to lose the command and distribute the control. [2]

IDEALISTIC VERSUS NATURALISTIC CHANGE

Traditional change models follow an *idealistic* path. This tends to be top-down and includes an unrealistic assumption of control, with an idealized end-state that you are aiming for. Most change initiatives you have been part of probably fall into this category, and you may be cynical about their capacity to shift a culture and change habits on a large scale and in the long term.

In recent years there has been growing interest in an alternative *naturalistic* path to change. This approach draws on an understanding of how emergent change happens in complex systems, from the weather to epidemics. [3]

QUICK FIX OR DEEP CHANGE

Change driven from above is easier to organize. It can also start delivering results more quickly and be more easily understood than *naturalistic* change, which can seem fuzzy and uncomfortable to people who don't like ambiguity (that's most people, then). Quick results can lead to improvements in morale. But eventually, top-down change initiatives will lose momentum because they depend on being pushed. Interest switches to other projects or leaders leave and progress stalls. [4]

GARDENERS NOT ENGINEERS

Naturalists believe, like Peter Senge, that 'to understand the process of change, we must think less like managers and more like biologists.' You can re-engineer machines. You can't re-engineer human organizations. At the core of the *naturalistic* approach is the belief that the machine age is over and we are in the age of the *human organization*. Therefore, old industrial methods of control, on which most top-down change initiatives are based, no longer work.

The loss of deference to authority is now well documented. The naturalists argue that the resistance to top-down change that results from this evaporation of authority means participative change models that *construct the future together* [5] are the long-term approach to raising organizational performance.

AND, FINALLY … TOUCH PEOPLE

If you are trying to lead major change, you need to go beyond logical arguments and touch people's feelings:

> *'Changing people's behaviour has a lot less to do with giving them analysis than it has to do with showing them something that is a truth that hits their feelings, which in turn shapes their behaviour. Now, I don't know about you, but that wasn't something I was taught when I was a young MBA student or a young professional, and it's a* **BIG DEAL.** *'*
> John Kotter

USEFUL CONCEPT

Epiphany: An epiphany is felt rather than thought. It is a *Eureka!* moment of the heart. Recent work on the neuroscience of change suggests we need as individuals and collectively to go through epiphanies in order to break redundant work patterns and embrace change. See the next *60 Second Leader Tale* for insights from **Renee Mauborgne** and **W. Chan Kim** on how to trigger epiphanies. And see Chapter 13, *Questions*, for more on the latest findings in the neuroscience of leadership and change.

SOURCES AND FURTHER READING

(1) *The Ultimate Business Library: 50 books that made management,* a great distillation book by Stuart Crainer with foreword and commentary by Gary Hamel.

(2) *Built to Change.* Don't manage change, create a change-ready company, argue Edward Lawler and Christopher Worley.

(3) 'Bramble Bushes In A Thicket', a paper by Dave Snowden and Cynthia Kurtz. I was going to fill this chapter unenthusiastically with John Kotter's 8-step change framework and references to Edgar Schein and other well-rehearsed territory, until the ever-prescient Johnnie Moore (*www.JohnnieMoore.com*) put me on to the paper by Snowden and Kurtz, and Patricia Shaw's book (see note 5).

(4) *The Dance of Change*, Peter Senge (see also *Presence*, by Senge).

(5) *Changing Conversations in Organizations: A Complexity Approach to Change*, Patricia Shaw.

A 60 Second Leader Tale: How to trigger epiphanies

A group epiphany can deliver a tipping point change in how people think and behave (see *Useful concept*, above, for why epiphanies are so important). **Renee Mauborgne** and **W. Chan Kim** argue that to trigger an epidemic movement of positive energy with limited resources, the key is to concentrate your leadership efforts on identifying and hitting 'kingpins' – as in the main pin that you hit when bowling to knock over the other nine. Here are two examples from them – two 30-second stories of epiphany-like change and how to trigger it.

---

1   TIPPING POINT CHANGE AT *NYPD*

'The New York Police Department (NYPD), in two short years in the 1990s, transformed itself from the worst to the best police organization in America. William Bratton, the department's chief of police, had to motivate 35,000 police officers to do an about-turn in virtually everything they did.

The first step Bratton took was an odd one: he ordered all senior officers to take the subway system to work, banning them from using their cars to commute.

Most companies that want to wake up their organization to the need for radical change make their case by pointing to the numbers. But numbers simply don't cut it. To line managers, the case for change seems abstract and remote. To break the status quo, employees must be put face-to-face with the problem.

When New York senior police officers were told to stop commuting to work in cars and to take the "electric sewer" (the subway) instead, they immediately saw the horror citizens were up against – aggressive beggars, gangs of youths jumping turnstiles, jostling people and drunks sprawled on benches.

With that ugly reality, the officers could no longer deny the urgent need for change in their policing methods. Numbers are disputable and hardly inspiring or memorable. But putting your managers face-to-face with poor performance is shocking … It exercises a disproportionate influence on tipping people's cognitive hurdle.'

2   TIPPING POINT CHANGE AT *PHILIPS LIGHTING NORTH AMERICA*
Getting your people to remove their blinkers and see the business as it really is takes courage. This is particularly true of large organizations that have been successful for a long time, and ignore signals that their performance is slipping. Here's an example:

'*Philips Lighting North America* was a very proud company. So proud that the sales force were convinced they were doing a first-class job even though they weren't gaining market share and General Electric dominated the industry.

That's when the new business head had his sales force listen in on a phone conversation between himself and Bernie Marcus, the founder of *Home Depot*, the largest retail customer in the US lighting industry. On this occasion the cognitive "kingpin" that the head of sales was looking to hit was the entrenched assumption by the sales force that they were better than they actually were.

"So, Bernie," he said, "how is our sales force doing?" Marcus replied: "Your sales force?" (His voice rose to a near-shout.) "They never follow through with what they commit to, deliveries are late, quantities and styles are wrong. It's a disaster. There are only excuses, no corrective action."

A dramatic attitudinal and behavioural turnaround occurred fast, as there was no place left for the sales force to hide.'

Source: Renee Mauborgne and W. Chan Kim, writing on how to achieve 'Tipping Point Leadership' – making big change happen despite few resources. You can find the full texts in their article 'Tipped For The Top', *People Management* magazine, April 2003 and the *INSEAD Quarterly*, 2004. Mauborgne and Kim borrow the phrase from Malcolm Gladwell's book of the same name, of course.

LEADING PEOPLE

13. The 60 Second Leader and ...

QUESTIONS

Why leading by asking questions beats leading by telling.

Michael Abrashoff, commander of the battleship USS *Benfold,* turned around a poor-performing ship to make it, by all available measures, the best performing ship in the US Navy. Captain Abrashoff used to ask every member of his 300-strong crew these three questions:

1   What do you like most about working here?
2   What don't you like about working here?
3   If you were the Captain, what would you change? [1]

Finding solutions through using questions to direct our attention goes all the way back to **Socrates**. And there is plenty of evidence that leading by asking questions is more effective than leading by telling. [2] However, too many leaders don't like questions.

WHY LEADERS DON'T ASK QUESTIONS
The problem leaders have with questions derives from two related leadership misconceptions:

1   the need to appear infallible; and
2   the concept of the leader as troubleshooter or solution-finder.

There's a common third reason leaders don't ask questions: they fear they'll get an answer they don't like.

THE WRONG QUESTIONS

When formal leaders do ask questions, they commonly ask the wrong ones: 'Why haven't you achieved this target?' or 'What's wrong and who's to blame?' [3] Even the Socratic method can backfire when wielded by someone in authority who practises flagellation by questioning.

Half-smart leaders half get it. They phrase instructions as questions, trying to lead people by the nose to the solutions the leader wants. But questioning as a disguised form of persuasion is a sham exercise and everyone knows it.

QUESTIONS CAN SPARK EPIPHANIES

David Rock and **Jeffrey Schwartz**'s recent work on the *neuroscience of leadership* points up how people buy into change. The brain's circuitry physically changes as new pathways are created, and our perception of reality alters. This generates a burst of gamma radiation in the brain and a rush of neurotransmitters like adrenaline – the 'Aha!' moment.

But, the change has to come from within, not from without. Questions allow us to reflect and arrive at the conclusion that the change is necessary and possible. That conclusion happens suddenly, appearing as a spark, a moment of epiphany or 'insight', as Rock labels it (I prefer epiphany). By contrast, when we are told a change is necessary, the brain resists, no matter how logical the argument for change might seem to the person putting it. [4]

GOOD QUESTIONS UNCOVER REALITY

Sidney Finkelstein says companies that are unable to question their prevailing view of reality are zombies. A zombie company, he says, is 'a walking corpse that just doesn't know that it's dead – because this company has created an insulated culture that systematically excludes any information that could contradict its reigning picture of reality.' [5]

WHAT MAKES A GREAT QUESTION?

Michael Marquardt tells us succinctly what makes a great question:

> *'Great questions are selfless, not asked to illustrate the cleverness of the questioner or to generate information or an interesting response for the questioner. They're generally supportive, insightful and challenging. They're often unpresumptuous and offered in a sharing spirit. Great questions are asked at a time when they generate the strongest amount of reflection and learning.'* [6]

Marquardt also gives the following examples of questions leaders may find useful:

- What is a viable alternative?
- What are the advantages and disadvantages you see in this suggestion?
- Can you more fully describe your concerns?
- What are your goals?
- How would you describe the current reality?
- What are a few options for improvement?
- What will you commit to do, by when?

A couple of those are a bit uninspiring and bloodless, I feel. I prefer the expansiveness of a question like 'What way forward can you see?'

'WHY?' QUESTIONS HAVE THE MOST POWER

Ricardo Semler, author of the book *Maverick* [7] and head of *Semco,* the Brazilian group of companies, says that the most important question for everyone to ask is 'Why?' and that it should be used to drill down at least three layers to ensure the foundation reasoning beneath any practice, procedure or decision is firm. At *Toyota,* employees are taught to drill down even further, asking 'why' consecutively five times.

USEFUL CONCEPT

The power of 'What if ...' thinking: 'Why ...' questions challenge existing practices. Conversely, 'Why not ...' and 'What If ...' questions open up discovery and innovation. By encouraging people to ask 'why?' and act on their answers, you are allowing them to think for themselves instead of trying to provide answers for them. And that's the essence of leadership. It's taken a couple of hundred years, but **Kant**'s summing up of the Enlightenment into three words – '*Think for yourself*' – has spread to every corner of the workplace.

SOURCES AND FURTHER READING

(1) Kevin Freiberg told me this and led me to Mike Abrashoff's book *It's Your Ship: Management Techniques From The Best Damn Ship In The Navy.*

(2) The *Center for Creative Leadership* studied 191 successful executives and concluded the key to success was creating opportunities to ask questions, and asking them. (**Source**: Michael Marquardt's book – see (6) below).

(3) Mike Harris, founding CEO of *First Direct* bank, says 'What's wrong?' and 'Who's to blame?' are the most destructive questions a leader can ask.

(4) *Quiet Leadership,* David Rock and *Appreciative Inquiry,* David Cooperrider.

(5) *Why Smart Executives Fail,* Sidney Finkelstein.

(6) *Leading with Questions: How Leaders Find the Right Solutions by Knowing What to Ask,* Michael J. Marquardt.

(7) See *Maverick* and *The Seven Day Weekend,* Ricardo Semler.

A 60 Second Leader Tale: Leading change by asking questions

This is one of the most interesting approaches to leading big change I have come across:

Farrelly Facilities and Engineering is a medium-sized firm based in the UK's West Midlands. **Gerry Farrelly** calls himself Director of Training. He's actually one of the twin brothers that started the company, but if you look at the job chart, neither of them calls himself Managing Director. In fact, no one does.

Gerry used questions to act as a catalyst in getting people to change how they and the organization worked. This is how he did it:

'Back in 1998 I realized I didn't enjoy what I was doing. I came across a study in one of the national newspapers that said something like 21 per cent of people enjoy going to work. People blamed bad management and long hours ... for a whole host of things happening in their personal lives such as break up of marriages, stress at home, no time to reflect, no time to read, basically no time for themselves.

Our catalyst for doing business differently was a dawning awareness that the company's employees fell into this category of seeing their jobs as grim, dogged struggles; that they were among the 80 per cent of employees who do not enjoy work.

I wanted to create a great company that would perform far better and bring people into work with a spring in their step and pride in what they do. I realized if I wanted my company to change like that the first thing I had to do was change myself. So I set myself a task: I would make a commitment to myself that if I wanted a better life – and it's not about money – if I wanted a better life and to enjoy my job, then I would change first.

I decided I would start a one-year programme of revisiting my values and then rebuilding everything I did so that I was living those values.

I asked the people who work with me to help me define those values. Basically, I told them I was dissatisfied with work and had decided I was going on a journey of change for a year to find a better, more fulfilling way of living and working. *I asked them if they wanted to join me to help find the answers.*

As part of this journey, I asked my staff what they wanted, how they saw life, how they saw their jobs. What I discovered on my journey was that no one wanted managing. Sure we need managers. But, people don't like to be told what to do. They wanted ownership of their jobs. They wanted ownership of their lives. What I discovered is that the Boss is dead.

We set about changing the whole culture of the business in 1998 to introduce fun, enjoyment, empowerment, leadership from the bottom – to mention just a few changes. We defined our purpose as to turn the enterprise into a 'Happiness Centred Business'.

Difference comes from the way people think rather than what you make. Our people differentiate themselves in part by operating in territory that competitors fail to occupy: the emotional economy. Our *Six Basic Rules of Heroes* that are practised throughout *Farrelly* are: empathy, social skills, motivation, self-regulation, self-awareness and emotional skills.'

The company's turnover doubled in three years, profits tripled and *Farrelly* employees now describe themselves in their company literature, which they write themselves, as 'among the happiest on this planet.'

One of the sources of inspiration that the people at *Farrelly* used to change how they work is the ancient Chinese text the *Tao Te Ching*, from which they selected this principle to guide everything they do:

'Working, yet not taking credit; leading yet not dominating. This is the primal virtue.'

Source: Gerry was speaking at a session of *The Inspired Leaders Network*, where the author was a director for a number of years. More on Gerry and the company here: *www.farrellyfacilities.com.*

14. The 60 Second Leader and ...

ATTENTION

Who's the spotlight on? You or them?

Leaders are too often at the centre of their own story, seeing themselves as the heart or head of the business unit they lead. Dream on. Half the time they are not even paying attention to you. And that's as it should be. As Jack Welch supposedly said about *GE* before he became CEO, its people spent too much time with 'their face to the boss and their ass to the customer.'

I heard the HR VP of *Microsoft UK* say a while ago that his main challenge was how to get the most out of brilliant young people who have a lot of knowledge but 'the attention span of a gnat'. To varying degrees, that's the challenge facing all leaders today – holding the attention of the people you are supposed to lead. Put it the other way around: if you can hold people's attention and thereby influence their behaviour, then you are a leader, whatever your job title.

Today's workers tend to pay attention to what they are interested in. And if that isn't you, it doesn't matter what your job title is or that you're their boss. You might appear to get their attention. But, while nodding at your pronouncements, they are probably really thinking about the problem they left on their desk or what they should cook for dinner tonight.

IT'S *NOT* THE INFORMATION ECONOMY

Michael Goldharber, the former theoretical physicist, unlocked this conundrum. We use phrases like *'the information economy'* and *'the knowledge economy'* because both these things are in more plentiful supply and circulation than ever before, he noted.

But power doesn't flow in the direction of information. It flows in the reverse direction – the attention being paid to the information is where the power is. Economics is about scarcity and value. We are awash with information and knowledge. Attention is the scarce commodity. So, we're actually in the Attention Economy. [1]

YOU GET ATTENTION BY GIVING IT

You can't inspire and lead people without earning their attention. You achieve that in a counter-intuitive way – by paying close attention to what interests them.

Robert Stephens is the brilliant young founder of the computer repair company *The Geek Squad*. He told me recently, when I was chairing his presentation to a conference, that his employees spend much of their off-time playing online computer games with each other. These are remote games where the players can be at great distances from each other but chat while they are playing. He observed them and noticed that they intersperse their game chat with work chat in which they swap tips on how to fix technical equipment.

Work and play merge with many knowledge workers. The border between the two is porous. So, Robert says he is looking to tap into their interest in online game-play by getting them to develop a game for themselves that acts as a form of training. He doesn't lead them away from where their interest and passion is. He doesn't compete with it for their attention. He leads them by tapping into **where their attention already is**. Simple but brilliant.

'Many of you want to be leaders, to make a difference. But you might be spending too much time self-marketing and not enough time researching, building bridges by taking an interest in someone … In true leadership situations, where a good coach/visionary is called for, listening comes before arm waving.'
Yahoo's Tim Sanders, blogging on *www.execubooksblog.com*

The Attention Economy: It's not the Information Economy. Attention is the scarcity item. You get people to pay attention to you as a leader by paying attention to their passions, interests and needs.

AND, FINALLY ... DALE GOT THERE FIRST

As Dale Carnegie put it, [2] 'You can make more friends in two months by becoming interested in other people than you can in two years by trying to get other people interested in you.' The same principle applies to attention and leaders.

SOURCES AND FURTHER READING

(1) *The Attention Economy*, Michael Goldharber. This is cited more for reference than as a reading suggestion. Goldharber's thesis is presented in the context of how the Web works. I've just adapted it and applied it to leadership in an age of information overload.

(2) *How To Win Friends And Influence People*, Dale Carnegie.

A 60 Second Leader Tale: Abe Lincoln's folded piece of paper

This is from Robert K. Cooper's great book *The Other 90%*. It's a story about Abraham Lincoln that tells us (a) how we all need acknowledgement and praise to bolster our confidence (even Lincoln did), and (b) how great leaders are out there where their employees and customers are, not locked away in a head office.

'When Daniel Boorstin, a noted historian and Librarian of Congress, was asked to name the most interesting thing he had ever found in the nation's capital, his answer was immediate – a small box containing the contents of Abraham Lincoln's pockets from the night he was assassinated: a pair of scratched eyeglasses, a very small amount of money, a pocket-knife, and a tattered but carefully folded newspaper clipping.'

The clipping noted that he worked, often alone, late into each night at the White House, seeking ways to save lives on both sides of the battle that raged day after day. His goal, the reporter wrote, was that the country would be able to heal itself at war's end.

Despite the pressures of his office, he made himself accessible to average citizens in a way no modern president would. Mothers with missing sons, wives with imprisoned husbands, and thousands of other people with personal tragedies petitioned this sensitive man. In his speeches, he constantly strove to convey an eloquence that was both anonymous and intimate: the plain, weighty tonality of his expressions was meant to feel as if it spoke in a voice already inside each of us.

The soldiers of the Union Army came through experience to know Lincoln. They knew, for instance, that after formal reviews he could be counted upon to wander among them telling humorous stories, despite the fact that at many times, as one private put it, "every lineament of his countenance indicated a severe mental and emotional strain."

Lincoln earned trust from soldiers because he did not view the world from behind his presidential desk, but through the eyes of those whose fears, hopes and humanity were caught up in that terrible war of brother against brother. Such empathy not only helps build trust, it opens you to new understandings and new possibilities. The voyage of discovery, as Proust said, depends not on visiting distant shores but on seeing the world with new eyes.

What set those specific, albeit modest, words of praise apart was that they spoke plain language about a distinctive effort Lincoln was making. Nothing grandiose – which was how he saw himself: an average human being committing everything he had to do a job well done.

How ironic that a small, "pathetic" piece of paper was a key to sustaining a man as great as Lincoln.'

Source: *The Other 90%: How to unleash your vast untapped potential for leadership and for life*, Robert K. Cooper.

15. The 60 Second Leader and …

STORIES

You have three stories to tell. Here's what they are.

Howard Gardner, in his book *Leading Minds,* says: 'The key to leadership is obtaining buy-in to the stories you tell and propagation of those stories'. [1]

This is true on at least three levels. Great leaders:

1   Tell a compelling story about **themselves**: who they are, where they come from, what they stand for, what they expect.
2   Create or tell a compelling story about **the organization**: its mission and purpose, why it is a great place to work, invest in and buy from.
3   Make **people** feel an essential part of the story through the work they do every day.

YOUR STORY

All leadership is autobiography. People want to know who you really are before they will accept you as a leader. You don't tell that personal story with just words. If you stop and chat with the doorman and show them as much respect and interest as you do the finance director, that will get around the organization and be part of your personal story – their sense of who you are.

The story you tell and the stories that people tell about you need to be authentic. But stories told about leaders are not always literally true. There's a great story people in the airline industry tell about Continental Airlines CEO Gordon Bethune, who witnessed a passenger being rude to a flight attendant as a plane was boarding. Bethune asked the abusive passenger how much his ticket cost. Then he took the cash out of his own pocket, paid him back and threw him off the plane. Before it had taken off, that is.

It's a great story. But, it never happened. People in the airline industry still circulate it in emails, even though they know it didn't happen, because Bethune has a reputation as a boss who fights for his people's interests. So the story maintains its currency because it's *the kind of thing he would do*. What's your personal story? What authentic stories do people tell each other about you?

YOUR COMPANY STORY

'The companies that will win in the future will be those with the best stories,' says Danish futurist Rolf Jensen. [2]

That doesn't mean projecting an image through marketing and advertising. It means the stories spontaneously generated by a company's actions – stories that attract people to want to work for you and be a customer.

Consumers are increasingly resistant to the marketing stories organizations tell about themselves. Instead, they listen to each other. Hence the growing power of customer advocacy and recommendation. It is viral stories, spread by customers and based on how the company behaves, that become your company story – not the stories put out by your PR people. [3]

THEIR PART IN THE STORY

Remember this mythical JFK anecdote? The President was visiting NASA headquarters and stopped to talk to a man with a mop. 'And what do you do?' he asked. 'I'm helping to put a man on the moon, sir,' said the janitor. Knowing their part in your company story engages people and gives them a sharp sense of purpose.

David Armstrong runs a $100 million freight company. New people at Armstrong's don't receive a policy manual, just a book full of stories about employees using their initiative to get things done.

Armstrong used to put these stories on an intranet – stories like the person he found on a loading bay at 3am doing the supervisor's job because the supervisor had been delayed. The point is to say, 'Here is a mortal like you: this is what we do. Read this as your training. Then act like this.'

Communicating internally through stories is more memorable than policies. Policies are words. Stories are about behaviours and actions. [4]

USEFUL CONCEPT

MBSA: Management By Walking Around, or MBWA, was brought to mass attention in the 1980s by Tom Peters and Bob Waterman, when they wrote about how it is used at Hewlett-Packard. Peters sometimes says in his seminars that twenty-five years later leaders need to learn to practise MBSA or Management By Storying Around.

SOURCES AND FURTHER READING

(1) *Leading Minds: An Anatomy of Leadership,* Howard Gardner.

(2) *The Dream Society,* Rolf Jensen.

(3) *Unleashing The Ideavirus,* Seth Godin; *The Cluetrain Manifesto,* Various.

(4) *The Leader's Guide to Storytelling,* Stephen Denning.

A 60 Second Leader Tale: Making people part of the story

In a large organization, how do you make everyone feel part of the story rather than just an anonymous cog in the machine?

There's a UK company called *Yell*. It produces the *Yellow Pages* directories among other things. It's a £1 billion-plus company with thousands of employees.

I met the communications director once, when Yell had 3,750 employees. He told me that the CEO used these three mechanisms as part of his commitment to make everyone part of the Yell story:

1   Everyone is in the book

The company produced a booklet on a regular basis, featuring targets achieved and targets to aim for. Everybody received a copy of the book. But, also, everybody was in the book, literally. The names of all 3,750 employees were included in the book as a roll of honour. When the books were handed out in an office, the first thing that would happen, almost ritualistically, is that everyone's head would be down as they riffled through the pages looking for their own name. Many of the employees would take the booklet home to show their family – 'Look: that's me.'

2   Everyone is part of the whole

The CEO also used a telling piece of language. He would constantly describe the company as a jigsaw puzzle made up of 3,750 pieces, each with a passion for excellence. One missing piece – one person not behaving with a passion for quality – spoils the whole. Yell is the only company to have won the *European Quality Award* (modelled on the Malcolm Baldrige national quality award in the US) twice.

3   The CEO meets everyone

The CEO also had an annual schedule designed to allow him to meet every employee at least once during the year, including holding long Q&A sessions with them. Candid Q&As are a powerful way to include people and make them feel part of the story. Sam Walton, Wal-Mart founder, also used to hold marathon Q&A sessions, but this time with thousands of shareholders in a football stadium especially hired for the occasion. Sam would take questions for SIX HOURS.

16. The 60 Second Leader and …

MOTIVATION

The three things people want. You are the incentive scheme.

Most motivation and incentive programmes are control-based systems. But **Aidan Halligan**, until recently Deputy Chief Medical Officer for England, said to me once, 'You can't injunct motivation and harness it to your plan. Motivation is intrinsic.'

HIRE FOR ATTITUDE, TRAIN FOR SKILL

Incentives tend to get people to chase bonuses and targets (see Chapter 18, *Targets*), skewing motivation towards gain rather than doing the job well. Hence a renewed focus in recent years on hiring people who are innately motivated rather than trying to build it in post-recruitment.

Robert Spector, who has analyzed the success of the *Nordstrom* department store and its legendarily motivated employees, asked a member of the *Nordstrom* Board once, 'Who trains your people?' 'Their parents,' was the immediate reply. [1]

The most successful *Nordstrom* salespeople can earn huge bonuses. But, the structure of their incentive system is not controlling. They are free to be as successful as they want, almost acting like independent franchisees who happen to be based in the *Nordstrom* store.

THE THREE THINGS PEOPLE WANT

The consultants *McKinsey* asked people 'What makes for a fantastic work environment?' [2] The three top answers were:

1   It's honest and open: 'I can trust my boss'.
2   I'm stretched: 'If I'm not there, I know I'll be missed'.
3   Risk – the ability to make decisions. 'Don't give me tasks. Let me make decisions.'

The **control** that *Nordstrom* and other high-performing organizations give their people over how they deliver shows up as number three.

YOU ARE THE INCENTIVE SCHEME

Incentive schemes designed to change your people's behaviour through control and rewards are just a proxy, a substitute for lack of meaning in the work itself. There's a far more powerful mechanism you can bring into play – the ability to inspire. That's why leadership is so important. As **John Kotter** puts it:

> *'Motivation and inspiration energize people, not by pushing them in the right direction as control mechanisms do, but by satisfying basic human needs for achievement, a sense of belonging, recognition, self-esteem, a feeling of control over one's life and the ability to live up to one's ideals. Such feelings touch us deeply and elicit a powerful response.'* [3]

RECOGNITION

Two words regularly top the polls when people are asked what they want more of from their boss: *thank you*. **Ken Blanchard** helped lead the charge on recognition and appreciation with his now widely preached (but not so widely practised) notion of *catching people doing things right* – reversing the manager's traditional role of policing – and publicizing that through mechanisms such as 'Eagle's nest' noticeboards (he has an anthropomorphic tendency to divide people into ducks and eagles).

Blanchard advises us to 'Forget all those artificial "employee of the month" initiatives. They just encourage the attitude that "So-and-so won it last month; it's the sales department's turn this month," which breeds cynicism.' [4]

USEFUL CONCEPT

The Law of Great Expectations: [5] Roger Bannister said, when asked how he broke the 4-minute mile, 'It's the ability to take out of yourself more than you've got'. If you make it clear to people you know they are capable of great things and provide the environment and resources they need to achieve, they will often surprise themselves by delivering more than they thought they could. It's the leader's faith in people that pump-primes the latter's own faith, if you like.

This faith is at its most powerful when it is specific and personal rather than generalized – when you know someone intimately and they feel you can see some capability in them that they were not fully aware of themselves. You need to **engage** with people to achieve that level of intimacy. They need to feel they know you and, if possible (with large organizations, not always possible), vice versa. Which is why our next chapter is on engagement.

SOURCES AND FURTHER READING

(1) *The Nordstrom Way*, Robert Spector.

(2) Rene Carayol at *www.carayol.com.*

(3) 'What Leaders Really Do', John Kotter, *Harvard Business Review.*

(4) Ken Blanchard, co-author of *The One Minute Manager*, *Raving Fans* and other works, was talking at the *European Conference on Customer Management* in London, 2005. The quotes, above, are from my notes.

(5) *The Feiner Points of Leadership: The 50 Basic Laws that Will Make People Want to Perform Better for You*, Michael Feiner. Feiner just calls it 'The Law of Expectations'. I added the 'Great' as I come from the land of Dickens and he doesn't.

A 60 Second Leader Tale: Handy on motivation

Charles Handy tells how he was trying to write one day and was suffering from writer's block. A group of children came by and were playing outside his window.

For some reason, the sounds unleashed his creative juices and the words started flowing. He went out to them, told them how great it was to hear them having fun outside his window, how it helped him work. Then he asked if they could come back the next day. They did. Same thing happened. So, he asks them back again.

At the end of the third day, he has got loads of work done to the sound of these kids playing outside his window and runs out, delighted. 'Come back tomorrow and I'll give you a pound!' he cries, triumphantly. That's about US$2 at the time of writing.

Next day: no kids. Handy finds his creative muse has disappeared with them. He goes off in search and finds the kids playing in another street. 'Why didn't you come back?' he asks.

'For a pound, it wasn't worth it,' is the scathing answer he gets.

I came across that story the other day and it reminded me how reward and recognition programmes can cheapen motivation and backfire unless they are carefully tailored to what actually makes your employees tick. I heard the story originally from **Frank Douglas**, a brilliant HR VP at Shell whose thinking and work I admire.

Leaders spend a lot of time and effort trying to motivate and animate people. Motivation and incentive programmes always seem completely uninspiring to me, a kind of papering over of the cracks, an admission that the substantive work in itself is not motivating enough. So, let's take a 60 second look at *Engagement* next, as it is the essential foundation for developing a motivated group of people.

17. The 60 Second Leader and ...

ENGAGEMENT

You don't want loyalty. The sixth discipline. The one-firm firm.

Fred Reichheld, the godfather of the loyalty movement, says that employees lingering with you for a long time may look like loyalty but is often in fact dead wood that has found a comfortable resting place. [1]

YOU DO WANT ENGAGEMENT BECAUSE

The *Gallup Organization* has virtually claimed this territory for itself with its long-running annual *Q12* employee engagement survey, [2] which proves conclusively that engaged employees are (a) in the minority, and (b) the only employees you need because of their far higher levels of commitment and performance.

By 'engaged' *Gallup* and others mean emotionally committed and involved rather than just going through the motions. Engaged people care about getting it right. *Gallup*'s survey finds consistently that maybe 70 per cent of the workforce is not engaged. They might be turning up for work but, psychologically, many of these people have already quit.

ENGAGEMENT COMES FROM DIALOGUE

Many people achieve extraordinary things outside work, but switch their internal lights off as they walk in the door to work. A critical role for a leader is to engage people so the extraordinary things many of them do outside work can be matched by an extraordinary them that comes to work.

Frank Douglas, an HR VP at Shell whose thinking I respect, says that for engagement to take hold, you need to develop a corporate conversation; a constant internal dialogue that builds understanding at all levels. [3] This dialogue needs to be an authentic internal conversation, not just an annual employee survey plus a series of employee relations initiatives based on the CEO making pronouncements. See the *Southwest Airlines* blog [4] for an example of how genuine internal communication can reinforce a culture of engagement.

THE SIXTH DISCIPLINE

The essential action of leaders and managers occurs almost entirely in conversations, noted the Australian leadership thinker **Alan Sieler**. *Conversation* is the sixth discipline that leaders need to develop if they are going to connect on a deep enough level to lead effectively. [5]

In terms of personal engagement, the most important leaders are line managers. People are engaged by or quit their direct superior. **Tim Rutledge**, in his book on engagement, [6] says there are three types of manager. Engaged managers (the only ones that concern us here) include these elements in their leadership conversation:

'[They] … recognize and accept that the whole person shows up for work and they engage with the whole person by:

1   *Chatting briefly and occasionally about family, vacations, weekends, good food, lousy movies and other matters.*
2   *Asking for their employees' help when they need it.*
3   *Not portraying themselves as infallible.*
4   *Helping their employees with their tasks when they're swamped.*
5   *Giving informal performance feedback in addition to formal appraisal.*
6   *Recognizing employee contributions in ways that are meaningful to the employee.*
7   *Providing opportunities for learning and development.*
8   *Providing career management support.*
9   *Providing a clear line of sight that links the employee's work with an organizational objective.'*

THE ONE-FIRM FIRM: ENGAGING AND VALUES

The brilliant David Maister reminds us, however, that the highest-performing organizations engage people with shared principles, not just the personalities and practices of individual leaders.

In 1985, Maister wrote an article for the *Sloan Management Review* called 'The One-Firm Firm,' which turned out to be one of their best-selling reprints. It identified a strategy common to leading firms across a broad array of professions for creating institutional engagement and team focus. He uses the word 'loyalty' instead of 'engagement', but we'll let him get away with it because he's brilliant:

'Loyalty in one-firm firms … is based primarily on a strong culture and clear principles rather than on the personal relations or stature of individual members. The key relationship is that of the individual member to the organization,' he writes.

'A contrasting, and more common, approach … is the *star-based* or *warlord* approach, which succeeds by emphasizing internal competition, individual entrepreneurialism, distinct profit centres, decentralized decision-making and the strength that comes from stimulating many diverse initiatives driven by relatively autonomous operators. The rainmakers of the firm are the warlords, and their followers, the mercenaries, are doing it for the money. Which would you bet on to win? In which environment would you want to work?' [7]

SOURCES AND FURTHER READING

(1) An interview between **Fred Reichheld** and **Phil Dourado.**

(2) *www.gallupconsulting.com.*

(3) *On Dialogue,* a book by David Bohm.

(4) I'm grateful to Johnnie Moore (www.johnniemoore.com) for pointing me at this: *www.blogsouthwest.com.*

(5) Writing in the magazine *Management Accounting,* Synan and Black noted this: 'Peter Senge, in his book *The Fifth Discipline,* popularized the idea that organizations can be seen as systems with their own internal logic … It may be useful to ask "What do people do in organizations?" … Managers spend 63–69 per cent of their time in conversation. If we could develop a foundation discipline based on conversation, it might become the much sought-after sixth discipline.'

(6) *Getting Engaged: The New Workplace Loyalty,* Tim Rutledge. Available from *www.gettingengaged.ca* for $29.95 Canadian.

(7) Maister's article is about professional services firms in particular, but much of it is widely applicable across sectors.

A 60 Second Leader Tale: Buckingham on engagement

The former *Gallup* employee Marcus Buckingham, with his best-selling (co-written) books [1] is a great source of insight into why you need an engaged workforce and how to get one. Here's a story I heard him tell on how great line leaders engage people:

ENGAGE PEOPLE WITH SPECIFICS

'When you ask average managers to talk about people, they talk in generalizations. Great managers don't make generalizations. Here's an example:

Rosa is in charge of a housekeeping team of thirteen at the *Hilton*, LA Airport. The average turnover of housekeeping staff in the hotel industry is 220–240 per cent a year. That's a complete change of people two to two and a half times a year. In practice, you have a core that remains and a rolling edge of people constantly leaving. The average tenure in Rosa's team, by contrast, is four and a half years.

Companies pay me to look at why variance in performance is huge across the same company, to look at the best performing areas of the company and analyze what is so good about them.

I asked Rosa about the housekeepers who worked for her and got no generalizations. I got stories. She told me about Lupita, for example. The housekeepers get 29 minutes to clean each room. Lupita is so organized she can do it in 27. So, whenever a fast turnaround is needed on rooms, Lupita is put on that job. Jennifer is a little slower, but she is a release valve for the team: when they have had a difficult time with a customer they get it off their chest with Jennifer.

Rosa also told me that another team member, Berta, is inquisitive and annoying; that the others find her sometimes abrasive, but that she is always looking for new ways of doing things and always asking "Why do we

---

have to do it this way?" Whenever Rosa wants to get a new project going she gives it to Berta.

So, when Rosa is managing Berta she spends 80 per cent of her time letting her use the best she's got to give. And she spends 20 per cent of her time managing around her abrasiveness.'

ENGAGE WITH PEOPLE'S STRENGTHS

'Most performance appraisals spend two minutes on what you do well and twenty eight minutes on "areas of opportunity" – your weaknesses! So, most conversations between managers and their people are around flaws and how to fix them. We live in a remedial world fascinated by weaknesses. That's wrong.

Think about the best manager you've ever had. They weren't soft on you. This isn't about being nice. They challenged you, pushed you, believed in your talent. They might even, in the extreme, have fired you because it was the wrong job for you, or counselled you out of a career move. The focus is always on you.

The best managers are able to see small increments in growth in performance in others, often providing the fuel you need to keep going.'

PEOPLE ARE NEVER FINISHED

'I know I'm not a great manager. I'm a focus person; I like working on a series of projects and finishing them one after the other. I don't like working in parallel. I found at Gallup that my work, which started off as one project, had mushroomed after 18 months into over a dozen projects, each with people working on them whom I was supposed to manage. I didn't like it. People are always *Work In Progress*. People are never finished. I know enough about great managers to know I can't do it. It's not that I'm not driven or smart enough. Great managers see people as an end. I see people as a means to an end.

The one thing you need to know about great managers is this: **find out what is unique about each person and capitalize on it.**'

Source: Notes taken by Phil Dourado from Marcus Buckingham's presentation to the annual *European Conference on Customer Management,* May 2006, London, organized by *www.ecsw.com.*

(1)   *First Break All The Rules* (written with Curt Coffman) and *Now Discover Your Strengths* (written with Donald Clifton, creator of the Clifton Strengthsfinder system). Buckingham's solo post-*Gallup* book, *The One Thing You Need To Know,* followed and built on the work of these first two. His latest book is *Go Put Your Strengths to Work.*

18. The 60 Second Leader and …

TARGETS

Look in the mirror. The Otis Redding problem.
Unplanned success.

> *'If I had to run a company on three measures, those measures would be customer satisfaction, employee satisfaction and cash flow.'*
> Jack Welch, former CEO of *GE*

LOOK IN THE MIRROR

If your organization and its people aren't performing, don't assume a new performance management and measurement system is what you need. Try looking in the mirror first.

Charles Dunstone, founder of *The Carphone Warehouse*, Europe's largest retailer of mobile phones, says: 'If your people aren't performing, assuming you are recruiting right, the first place you should look is yourself and the environment you put them in. My goal is to continue to squeeze more out of our people than they think they can give. Not in an exploitative way. It's a simple formula: clear values plus goals.'

Dunstone is not saying 'don't measure'. He's just saying be more clever about what you measure and how you do it. For example, he lets customers score his people:

'We are ferocious measurers of how we are doing. We send every single customer a satisfaction questionnaire and a thank you letter when they buy a phone. All the results are fed into a database. We run a very cruel thing called the hall of fame and the hall of shame. Every three months we print a list of every person within the company and the average score given to them by their customers. Nothing more is said – no rewards, no penalties, no punishments.' [1]

THE OTIS REDDING PROBLEM

Performance measurement systems based on targets are notoriously hard to design. One mistake many leaders make is to measure and reward people on too many dimensions. They end up pulled in so many directions the measurement system becomes useless.

Bob Sutton and **Jeffrey Pfeffer** call this *The Otis Redding Problem*, [2] after the line in the song 'Sitting On the Dock of the Bay':

'I can't do what ten people tell me to do.
So I guess I'll remain the same.'

Sutton says that's the problem with holding people, groups, or businesses to too many metrics: they can't satisfy or even think about all of them at once, so they end up doing what they want or the one or two things they believe are important or that will bring them rewards (regardless of senior management's strategic intent). [2]

The rise of balanced scorecards has made the problem worse. Though scorecards have value in moving managers' thinking from measuring the past to getting ready for the future, they often grow to encompass a ridiculously long list of metrics. Bob Sutton remarks that one banker proudly told him they had just added their 100th metric to their balanced scorecard. [3]

UNPLANNED SUCCESS

Performance measurement systems based on targets can also hold people back from discovering better ways of doing things, and they can take the focus away from unplanned successes. **Jim Clemmer** stresses that great leaders encourage and reward *unanticipated* results:

'During your reviews and assessments, be especially vigilant for unexpected and unplanned successes. Dig deeper to understand the unanticipated results. Often you'll find "happy accidents", chance changes, or highly effective championing behavior. These are key sources of innovation. Study, learn, and understand what's going on. Time spent figuring out how to replicate and spread the causes of these results can be just as productive as problem solving, gap analysis, or improvement planning.' [4]

USEFUL CONCEPT

Goodhart's Law: Named after a chief economist at the *Bank of England*. Goodhart's Law states that if a measure becomes a target it loses its value and ceases to be a measure. Controlling an indicator of a problem will not cure the problem. Goodhart himself phrased it like this: 'Any observed statistical regularity will tend to collapse once pressure is placed upon it for control purposes'. [5]

SOURCES AND FURTHER READING

(1) Charles Dunstone, in an interview with Phil Dourado.

(2) *The Knowing–Doing Gap*, Jeffrey Pfeffer and Robert Sutton.

(3) Bob Sutton's blog *www.bobsutton.typepad.com*.

(4) Leadership guru Jim Clemmer at *www.clemmer.net*.

(5) *Central Banking, Monetary Theory and Practice: Essays in honour of Charles Goodhart,* page 96. Systems thinking, as practised by *Toyota* and other high-performing organizations, stresses that target-based systems distort behaviour and make your organization inflexible.

John Seddon's book *Freedom From Command and Control* is helpful in understanding systems thinking and how you can lead more effectively by using it.

A 60 Second Leader Tale: What can't yet be measured doesn't get done

The vast majority of managers I have ever asked have agreed with and approved of the statement 'What gets measured gets done.' But, then the inverse must also be true: 'What can't yet be measured doesn't get done.' And this is the limiting factor built into an exclusively measurable approach to leading an organization.

Our second *60 Second Leader Tale* from **Captain Mike Abrashoff** of the USS *Benfold* illustrates how the law of measurability stifles creativity. Abrashoff is famous for taking a poor-performing ship with low morale and turning it into 'the best damn ship in the Navy', as it became known.

'I gave my first speech at a two-day conference sponsored by the magazine *Fast Company* to six hundred people … After I talked about *Benfold*, the questions began … The worst one was, "What kind of metrics did you use when you were determining where you wanted to go?"

I stood there like a deer caught in headlights. I was in such a hurry to change the way we did business that I had bypassed conventional business wisdom on how to implement change. The crowd tittered.

Later I called my sister Connie, who has an MBA and has worked for major financial institutions all over the country. She said the management committee always wants to see the metrics before they allow you to launch new ideas. Since, by definition, new ideas don't have metrics, the result is that great ideas tend to be stillborn in major companies today.

I just knew where *Benfold* was when I arrived and, generally, where I wanted us to go from there. If I had been forced to chart a course defined by metrics, the creativity we sparked and the changes we achieved probably could not have happened …'

Abrashoff's instinctive conclusion that 'What gets measured gets done' closes down your options has some powerful backers, including strategy guru **Henry Mintzberg**. 'Can you measure it?' as a golden rule leads, says Mintzberg, to a strong bias toward 'cost leadership strategies (emphasizing operating efficiencies, which are generally measurable) over product leadership strategies (emphasizing innovative design or high quality, which tends to be less measurable).' [1]

As Jack Welch used to say, the numbers are the outcome of great leadership. You don't lead by the numbers. The numbers emerge from the leadership. Abrashoff went on to prove this. Just months after creating a new regime in which he expected his crew to constantly come up with better ways of doing things rather than wait to be instructed in what to do, the ships measures started to climb.

'... just seven months after I took the helm, *Benfold* earned the *Spokane Trophy* ... It is given each year to the most combat-ready ship in the Pacific Fleet.

Shortly after the award was announced, my boss, the commodore, sent me an e-mail offering congratulations. But don't get too cocky, he warned. His ship had not only won the equivalent award in the Atlantic Fleet, it had also achieved the Navy's all-time highest score in gunnery: 103.6 (out of a possible 105). 'Until you can beat my gunnery score,' he wrote, "I don't want to hear any crowing from USS *Benfold*."

Two weeks later, we were scheduled to shoot our own gunnery competition. I didn't say a word to my team; I just taped that email to the gun mount. They scored 104.4 out of a possible 105, after which I let them write a response to the commodore ...

Benfold went on to beat nearly every metric in the Pacific Fleet, and frequently the crew broke the existing record. Directly, I had nothing to do with these triumphs. As I saw it, my job was to create the climate that enabled people to unleash their potential. Given the right environment, there are few limits to what people can achieve.'

Source: This *60 Second Leader Tale* is from Captain D. Michael Abrashoff's book *It's Your Ship: Management techniques from the best damn ship in the Navy.*

(1) *The Rise and Fall of Strategic Planning*, Henry Mintzberg.

DISTRIBUTED LEADERSHIP

19. The 60 Second Leader and ...

INNOVATION

The essential tension. Fast second. Mandate innovation.

Leading innovation is one of the least understood and most challenging areas of leadership. It's not about technology or research and development. It's about everything.

Successful innovation comes about at the intersection of experience and novelty. The two pull against each other and the leaders of organizations that want to foster innovation have to channel this tension into creativity. It's the grit that forms the pearl. **Thomas Kuhn**, the father of scientific thinking about innovation, taught us this. He called it *'the Essential Tension'.* [1]

MAKE YOUR PEOPLE THE GENIUSES

Scott Cook, founder of *Intuit*, a truly innovative firm, takes Kuhn's scientific thinking and coats it in business reality with his observation that 'innovation happens at the junction between business and customer needs.' Your existing business practices are the *experience or tradition* that Kuhn refers to. Emergent customer need – that customers themselves may be unconscious of – provides the *novelty*. You need to discern what the emerging, often half-formed novelty is, and adapt your business practices to satisfy that emergent need.

Cook says there are five models of innovation ... but that only one of them really works, for his company at least. They are:

1   The lone genius

2   The boss is a genius

3   Copy competitors' inventions

4   Cluster the geniuses in a lab

5   Make your people the geniuses (clue: it's this one). [2]

FAST SECOND?

But Scott Cook's discarded option three, above, works too. **Henry Ford** famously said the best business strategy is to be the first person to be second, once all the problems have shown themselves in a new technique.

That was sound advice in 1910 because then product life cycles were longer. Now, by the time you've decided to be second, you'll often have lost the market. Not always, however: in some sectors fast second is a sound risk reduction strategy. *Apple's* point-and-click *Graphical User Interface* came first. **Microsoft's** copy, *Windows*, was a fast second. We all know who won that one. [3]

MAKE AN IDIOT OF YOURSELF

Paradoxically, to allow people to be geniuses you have to let them be idiots. **Tom Peters** says that a commitment to innovation means being prepared to make an idiot of yourself. By that, he means allow your success rate to slip, and encourage others to do the same, by trying things that you do not know will work (see Chapter 1, *Failure*). This is counter-intuitive for most working cultures, which are built on predictability: repeating what you know works.

When **Lou Gerstner** ran Travel Related Services at *American Express*, before taking over *IBM*, he set up a $10 million 'play fund' for artificial intelligence (AI). The basic rules were that a project could claim up to $50,000 in seed funding as long as it was for a PC or Mac operating system. Each proposal had to be made on one page and was guaranteed to be approved or rejected within five days.

Gerstner's instructions were simple, says Peters: 'Screw around with AI and see what you come up with'. You only need one $25,000 project to become a several-million-dollar success story to win. '*Microsoft* is the perfect example of this *Ready Fire Aim* approach: they put out products full of imperfections and then work and work at them until the 180th version is perfect. If they had waited for the perfect version, the market would have gone elsewhere by the time they got there,' says Peters. [4]

USEFUL CONCEPT

Make innovation an expectation: **Edward de Bono** says that at the end of every meeting the chairperson must allocate the last fifteen minutes to anyone who is exploring a new idea. If no one has anything to say, they are told they are not doing their job. This process produces a creative hit list of new thinking, or can kick off the transfer of a new practice from one part of an organization to another. [5] Jack Welch at *GE* used to insist that every meeting included an exchange of new ideas or new techniques.

SOURCES AND FURTHER READING

(1) *The Structure of Scientific Revolutions*, Thomas Kuhn.

(2) Scott Cook was talking at *CHI 2006,* April 24 plenary session, Montreal, Canada.

(3) *Fast Second: How Companies Bypass Radical Innovation to Enter and Dominate New Markets*, Constantinos C. Markides, Paul Geroski.

(4) Tom Peters was speaking at ecsw.com's *North American Conference on Customer Management,* Florida, USA.

(5) Edward de Bono and Robert Heller's *Management Newsletter*, available from *www.thinkingmanager.com.*

A 60 Second Leader Tale: The Accidental Innovator – the power of the prepared mind

Leading innovation involves creating a culture where people look out for accidents and explore the benefits of them. This builds on the idea of accepting failure as something that you sift through to find the benefits of, rather than as something to be condemned.

It's widely known that Post-It notes emerged from a glue invented by 3M that didn't work. The creation of a product was retrospective, not intentional. It was accident turned into serendipity by what Pasteur called 'the prepared mind'.

ACCIDENTAL INNOVATIONS INCLUDE ...

- anaesthesia
- Cellophane
- cholesterol-lowering drugs
- cornflakes
- dynamite
- the ice cream soda
- ivory soap
- artificial sweeteners
- nylon
- penicillin
- photography
- rayon
- PVC
- smallpox vaccine
- stainless steel, and
- Teflon.

Robert D. Austin, who has studied accidental innovation, says that to lead innovation you have to draw from art as much as from science. Most organizations adopt a scientific model of innovation, as innovation thinking emerged from research and development, and tends to focus on new product development. But innovation throughout the enterprise in how work is done is the broader role that leaders have to develop.

Austin says he became interested in the subject when he was interviewing artists about their creative processes and found many of them to rely on accidents as a source of interesting and creative outcomes. He says: 'I would not really label this "accidental innovation." The innovation itself can't really be said to be "accidental," even though it involves accident. It takes a considerable capability to see the value in an accident, and to build upon it to create even more value.'

Austin notes that artists try to develop a talent for causing good accidents, and they cultivate an ability to notice the value in interesting accidents – what Pasteur called 'the prepared mind.'

Gary Hamel points out that watching how customers use products can lead to innovation. Webcams placed in student dorms to see how they used microwave ovens showed that a surprisingly large number used them to dry their pants after doing the laundry. A whole new generation of microwave-based clothes dryers emerged from this observation.

Text messaging, a mass consumer market in the UK, is an accidental market. I heard Charles Dunstone, CEO and founder of *The Carphone Warehouse*, explain once that the text messaging facility was only built into phones to allow engineers to relay fault status to customers. It was never intended as a customer-to-customer mass-market revenue-generator.

Sources: Robert D. Austin and Lee Devin's *Harvard Business School Working Knowledge* paper 'Accident, Innovation, and Expectation in Innovation Process'. Plus an interview between Gary Hamel and Phil Dourado.

20 The 60 Second Leader and ...

CULTURE

Culture change: ten things you can do. All culture is local.

> 'A woman cuts off the end of a ham before roasting it. When asked by her
> husband why she does that, she says that her mother always did it. It turns
> out that her mother's roasting pan was too small for a ham ... so that's what
> started the habit.'
> Donald Mitchell [1]

It's the leaders' lament. How can something as 'soft', invisible and elusive
as your corporate culture be so resilient that it will absorb change initiative
after change initiative and, just when you think you have made progress,
rebound back to its former shape? Here are ten things you can do ...

TEN THINGS YOU CAN DO

Edgar Schein, the world's leading corporate culture expert, looked at the
best techniques available to change a culture. His research produced the
following list, in descending level of significance: [2]

1   What official leaders attend to, measure, reward and control is the main
    factor affecting culture
2   How leaders react to critical incidents (do you or they get defensive, go
    on the attack, support, blame?)
3   Leader role-modelling and coaching
4   Criteria for recruitment, promotion and retirement
5   Formal and informal socializing
6   Recurring systems and procedures
7   Organizational design and structure
8   Design of physical space

9   Stories and myths about key people and events

10   Mission statements, charters and ethical codes

ALL CULTURE IS LOCAL

Workplace culture and performance experts like **Marcus Buckingham** point out that large organizations commonly have massive variance in culture across them. 'Companies don't have one culture. The day-to-day reality of working in a company varies from place to place within that company ... There are as many cultures as there are managers. People join companies but they quit bosses. Culture is local,' argues Buckingham. [3]

SUBCULTURES: UNCOVERING THE HIDDEN FACTORY

Buckingham is largely referring to the power of subcultures. The biggest mistake the official leaders at the top of an organization can make is to assume that the publicly stated corporate version of your culture – vision, values, processes, brand statements and so on – is in fact the dominant culture throughout the organization. Often the official culture exists only on paper.

In the 1980s the disparity between official manufacturing processes and what actually went on in factories became clearer as manufacturing was reorganized to learn from Japanese methods. One senior manager at *GE* coined the phrase '*the hidden factory*' to refer to all the unofficial reworking that had gone on. Many workplace cultures today harbour their own kind of hidden factory.

Some sociologists have coined the phrase '*occupational consciousness*' to describe the groupthink culture that can emerge in working units. The sociologist **Laurie Taylor** explains: 'After the tricks of the trade have been learned, a new worker is slowly introduced to the culture of the workplace – all the ways in which this specific group of workers differentiate themselves from others in the same company, all the idioms and jargon which promote a sense of communality, all the defences and justifications which can be mustered when individuals in the group are under threat or attack.' [4]

USEFUL CONCEPT

UGRs or Unwritten Ground Rules: [5] The further away from the frontline and from actual worker and customer experience leaders are, the more likely the 'official' culture is to depart from reality. The resulting vacuum is filled with UGRs, which become dominant in defining your actual (unofficial) culture and the subcultures within it. You have to dig deep to identify UGRs and ensure the official culture is rooted firmly enough in reality to keep UGRs from taking over.

SOURCES AND FURTHER READING

(1) The ham story is from the book *The 2,000 Per Cent Solution* by Donald Mitchell.

(2) *Organizational Culture and Leadership*, Edgar Schein. This summary of ten of Schein's points is courtesy of Jay Bevington, Professor Aidan Halligan* and Ron Cullen who lead the *NHS Clinical Governance Support Team*, a group of leading change agents I admire enormously. *Aidan has just left the NHS, which is a great shame for that organization. See also Schein's book *Corporate Culture Survival Guide*.

(3) My notes from a talk given by Marcus Buckingham in May 2006, London.

(4) From Laurie Taylor's *Thinking Allowed* email newsletter, October 2006

(5) The Australian workplace culture consultant Steve Simpson has produced a book called *UGRs: Cracking The Corporate Culture Code*.

A 60 Second Leader Tale: Participative leadership

If you've read the previous two chapters, *Innovation* and *Culture*, I'm hoping you'll be in a receptive mood to spend 60 seconds exploring some innovative practice.

You may be familiar with the *Boeing*-inspired change approach of 'getting everybody into the same room'. In *Boeing*'s case, this meant literally getting 2,000 people into an aircraft hangar to help break down silos and give people a visceral sense of being part of a large group of people creating a common agenda for whole-organization improvement. The Boeing 777 airliner is said to be the direct result of this approach.

Critical-mass thinking, whole systems thinking, large group interventions ...

... a number of names have emerged to label the idea that you can have a meeting where everyone turns up and things get decided that can quickly shift the direction of a giant organization. But, whatever you call it, it's clearly a form of participative leadership. [1]

Open Space is a structured version of the 'whole-organization experience'. In this *60 Second Leader Tale* I'll leave it to an experienced *Open Space* facilitator (Lisa Heft) and a self-organizing information system (*Wikipedia*) to tell the tale of *Open Space* as a format for stimulating whole-organization leadership – where everyone can contribute to leading major change.

LISA HEFT

'*Open Space* originated because **Harrison Owen** designed and planned a conference, and when it took place he noticed that all the best work was done during the coffee breaks. All the networking, deal-making, visioning, and collaboration, all the new ideas and new products and new

---

programs, came from small circles of people chatting over similar passions and interests. Just as it happens in life. So for the next conference he designed a process that would be all coffee-break energy, all the time. Thus *Open Space Technology* was born.'

WIKIPEDIA

'**Open Space Technology (OST)** is, among other things, a way to convene people for a conference, retreat or meeting. "Technology" in this case means "tool"; a process, a method. This method has been used all over the world by thousands of practitioners for groups of people from 4 to over 2000.

At its least, OST is a meeting methodology. It is also a philosophy and a life practice. Its essential core is the invitation to take responsibility for what you have passion for. The remarkable outcome of this simple idea is that when participants do so, the needs of both the individual and the collective are met.

Open Space Technology enables groups of any size to address complex, important issues and achieve meaningful results quickly. It is at its best where more traditional meeting formats fail: when there is conflict, complexity, diversity of thought or people, and short decision times. It has been used in widely diverse settings, from designing aircraft doors at a large aircraft manufacturing company to engaging street kids in defining a sustainable jobs program.

Originated by Harrison Owen in 1986, Open Space has been used in over 100 countries and in diverse settings, industries, cultures and situations – for program and product design, knowledge exchange, interdisciplinary thinking, conflict resolution and conferences.'

'**The Law of Two Feet** – a foot of passion and a foot of responsibility – expresses the core idea of taking responsibility for what you love. In practical terms, the law says that if you're neither contributing nor getting value where you are, use your two feet (or available form of mobility) and go somewhere where you can. It is also a reminder to stand up for your passion. From the law flow four principles:

- Whoever comes is the right people.
- Whatever happens is the only thing that could have.
- Whenever it starts is the right time.
- When it's over, it's over.'

To explore *Open Space* further go to Lisa Heft's *www.openingspace.net*. Click on 'gallery' and be walked through how *Open Space Technology* works in an interesting visual storyboard.

I have no commercial connection with Lisa Heft or affiliation with *Open Space*. It's not proprietary; no one sells it. That's one of the things I find interesting about it. As with a number of the more forward-thinking leadership tools and methods mentioned in this book, Johnnie Moore (*www.Johnnie-Moore.com*), who is a practised facilitator in this field, introduced me to it.

Note: (1) *Critical Mass Interventions* (CMIs) evolved from early practices in the field of organization development in the 1950s. CMIs are part of the field of self-directed work that led to self-managed teams and other forms of self and peer leadership. The work of Fred Emery, Eric Trist and the *Tavistock Institute* with British coal miners is what led to the development of critical mass interventions. Organization development specialists will tell you that critical mass interventions are an example of a ***socio-technical system***.

21. The 60 Second Leader and ...

LEADING FROM THE MIDDLE

The layer of clay. Pyramids are tombs. 'Middle-up-down' change

THE LAYER OF CLAY

After a couple of decades of being bashed about and seen as expendable – stripping out middle managers is a favourite pastime among practitioners of 'Business Process Engineering' – the people left in the middle can feel overworked and squeezed by demands from above and below. **Sir Nick Scheele**, when he was put in charge of turning around *Ford of Europe*, says, 'I discovered that the middle managers were called by the people at the top "the layer of clay". How inspired to lead would you feel if that's how the rest of the organization saw you?' [1]

I hosted a seminar in 2002 to help mark the 20th anniversary of **Tom Peters** and **Bob Waterman**'s book *In Search of Excellence*. I say 'host'; I just introduced Tom Peters to his audience and he did the rest. Halfway through he paused to take questions. Here's what my notes say he answered to the first question:

Q: We're not the CEOs of our companies. So, how can we make the revolutionary changes to our organizations that you preach?

A: You convince the higher-ups of the need for change by doing it, not by brilliant PowerPoint presentations. Find common cause. Identify fellow freaks across your organization and work with them to make changes you can then show to the bosses *after* you have done it.

PYRAMIDS ARE TOMBS

If you are in the middle of a hierarchy and feel your ability to lead is stifled by lack of positional authority, then read one of the *60 Second Leader* recommended texts, Captain Mike Abrashoff's first book, which is cited several times in these pages. [2] Abrashoff points out that as captain of a ship of 310 people he was the equivalent of a middle manager in a large organization, hemmed in by layers of leaders above and 225 years of Navy rules. He broke many of the rules and pioneered new practices. If you can do that in a military hierarchy, then the hierarchy *you* are in can't be structurally more challenging, surely. Read his book to find out how.

Harvard Business School professor John Kotter argues that 'leaders must understand that leadership is not just a job of the person above them in the hierarchy ... the most common sort of leadership that you see today that is useful are (*sic*) people who challenge the status quo, vacuum up information from all directions, establish – by themselves or with others – a sense of direction, vision, for their little piece of the action, and then create some strategies for making the vision a reality.' [3]

MIDDLE-UP-DOWN CHANGE

Research shows that, without leadership from the middle, your organization will go nowhere. **Kjell Nordstrom** and **Jonas Ridderstrale** put it this way: 'Our experience is that often the best and most critical people sit in the middle. We only have to use them in the right way ... translating vision into action and action into vision. Many Japanese companies no longer talk about bottom-up or top-down processes. Instead, they realize that real organizational action is dependent on processes better characterized as middle-up-down.' [4]

USEFUL CONCEPT

The 360 Degree Leader: [5] John C. Maxwell, via his ghost writer Charlie Wetzel, says that how to lead down in an organization is foundational. But unprecedented concepts like how to lead horizontally across your peers and how to lead those to whom you report – leading upward – are revolutionary ideas in most organizations. These two behaviours – leading across and leading upward – are what sets apart organizations that genuinely practise good leadership today. And there are very few of them.

SOURCES AND FURTHER READING

(1) *Seven Secrets of Inspired Leaders,* Phil Dourado and Dr Phil Blackburn.

(2) *It's Your Ship,* Michael Abrashoff. Mike's follow-up book is called *Get Your Ship Together.*

(3) *The Leader's Digest,* Jim Clemmer. Jim also recommends on this subject the book *Getting Things Done When You're Not In Charge* by Geoffrey Bellman.

(4) *Funky Business,* Kjell Nordstrom and Jonas Ridderstrale.

(5) *The 360 Degree Leader,* John C. Maxwell (Charlie Wetzel). The advice in this book is a bit Zelig-like, for my liking (as in the character in the Woody Allen movie of the same name who moulds his personality to be a clone of the nearest strong character). It advises, for example, that if your boss likes golf, take it up so you can schmooze.

A 60 Second Leader Tale: True leaders feel their customer's pain

Sir Nick Scheele, till recently President and COO of *Ford Motor Company*, explains why leaders need to listen directly to the voice of the customer, without intermediaries.

> 'When I was in charge of *Jaguar*, I used to use the trip home to listen to tapes we had made of customers calling in with complaints. I remember driving home and cringing as I listened to one particular call.
>
> It was a woman describing how she had to climb out of the sun-roof of her car, in the pouring rain, slide down the windscreen and off the bonnet, because the electronic door locks of her Jaguar had seized up, trapping her in. You can imagine the state of mind she was in; the distress that our product had created. And it was only through hearing directly from the customer that I partially shared that state of mind, was allowed into it.
>
> It is common practice for senior managers to be shielded from customers, for middle managers to be intermediaries processing customer satisfaction ratings and market research findings and presenting them to the boss in a neatly bound report.
>
> If that is how you work, then you are not in touch with your customers, and therefore not in touch with the reality of your business. You have to hear direct from customers to realize where the critical path lies for improvements to your business. If you have intermediaries between you and your customers – your market – then you are too far removed ...'

At Amazon, CEO Jeff Bezos requested a weekly report on the issues customers were raising with customer service staff. This is now a standard tool within Amazon, known as WOCAS (What Our Customers Are Saying) reports. They go straight to the CEO, along with 'customer verbatims' – the actual emails sent in by customers – on any topic that Bezos wants to monitor.

As part of Xerox's turnaround in performance, its new CEO instigated a regime in which senior managers regularly take it in turns to take calls on the complaints phone lines. They are responsible for pursuing to resolution any complaints they receive, and for supervising a root cause analysis if the complaint is evidence of an underlying problem that needs to be fixed.

So, what does your organization do to keep its leaders up close and personal with customers?

22. The 60 Second Leader and ...

CUSTOMERS

'They serve like we lead.' Prosumption. The new Golden Rule.

'They serve like we lead,' said Sir **John Sainsbury**, founder of the UK supermarket chain. Research at *Harvard* in the 1990s [1] showed there is a measurable continuum running from inside your organization to outside, like a connecting thread. Treat people well, they in turn treat customers well, customer satisfaction goes up, profits go up. It's measurable, apparently. But, only *very* satisfied customers are loyal. And a more interesting offer from elsewhere can make them defectors overnight.

DESIGNING THE EXPERIENCE

Rather than simply selling products and services, you now need to move your organization up the hierarchy, stepping up their thinking from 'product' to 'service' to 'experience' as if moving up a staircase. [2] And your customers are players in this process, not recipients on the outside.

FROM 'CONSUMER' TO 'PROSUMER'

Alvin Toffler first coined the word 'prosumer' in 1979. Conflating the words 'producer' and 'consumer', Toffler used the new word to describe the next generation (this generation) of customer: one that is not just passive, but becomes involved in the production process. For evidence of prosumption in action you only have to stand in a *Starbucks* queue and listen to the customer in front tell the *barista* the specifications of the tall, skinny, dry latte with an extra shot of espresso that they want right now. The customer is designing their own coffee and telling the production department how to make it.

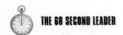

> 'Consumers did not have much share of voice. Now they do. There is a fundamental transition that is taking place – from a firm-centric society to a consumer-centric society.' [3]
> C. K. Prahalad

Moving toward 'co-creation' with customers involves a complete rethink of your strategy and operation. At its simplest, you move your thinking and structures from supplier 'push' (controlled from the top) to customer 'pull' processes (control moves to the edge), putting more initiative and decision-making power in the hands of the people who interact with customers. Think 'demand chain' instead of 'supply chain' and see how different the world looks from that perspective.

USEFUL CONCEPT

The NEW golden rule: 'We're always told to treat customers as we would want to be treated. That's not right. Treat customers as *they* want to be treated. Find out. Don't assume. The golden rule isn't "Do as you would be done by." It's "Do unto others as they would like to be done unto." **Source:** I heard this from Ken Pasternak, President, *Inter Associates Ltd*.

AND, FINALLY ... THE CUSTOMER IS *NOT* KING

Yes, over-supply means the balance of power has swung from supplier to customer. But don't believe the old cliché that every customer is king. Some are more trouble than they are worth. At *Southwest Airlines* a complaining customer had refused to be placated by every layer of management that her letters were escalated to and was threatening never to fly with the airline again. In desperation the file was bumped up to the only layer left, CEO **Herb Kelleher**. In five minutes Herb wrote a nine-word letter back to the customer, solving the problem. It said 'Dear Mrs ___ We will miss you. Love Herb.'

SOURCES AND FURTHER READING

(1) *The Service Profit Chain*, James Heskett, W. Earl Sasser, Leonard A. Schlesinger.

(2) *The Experience Economy: Work is Theatre and Every Business a Stage*, Joseph Pine and James Gilmore.

(3) *The Future of Competition: Co-Creating Unique Value with Customers*, Professors C. K. Prahalad and Venkatram Ramaswamy.

A 60 Second Leader Tale: Leaders on the frontline

Jan Carlzon, the turnaround CEO of *SAS Airlines* and author of the classic book for creating a customer-centred turnaround, *Moments of Truth,* likes to tell this story:

'I noticed a while back that the *Mandarin Oriental Hotel* in Hong Kong had won, for the second time running, a highly prestigious customer service award. The General Manager there was a friend of mine. So I called him up, congratulated him and asked him what his secret is.

"I don't know," he said. "Maybe it's because we give our frontline people the authority to say 'yes' to customers. But we don't give them the authority to say 'no'. If they feel they need to say 'no' to a customer request, they have to seek permission from their manager first."

If you want to make a real difference to customers, look at your approvals and permissions process to allow frontline people to take the initiative, to lead as they interact with customers. The more decisions have to be referred for approval, the more in danger your organization is because it's not going to be fast or flexible enough at the edges to be competitive.

23. The 60 Second Leader and ...

FRONTLINE LEADERSHIP (1)

Where should leaders be? Out in the business

It is fashionable to say that the more a leader works **in** the business, the less they can work **on** the business. The implication is that getting mired down in the detail of the organization prevents you from taking bigger decisions. This disdain for being in the business is not just slightly wrong, it's entirely wrong.

The UK retail billionaire **Philip Green** walks through his empty stores at night to immerse himself in the shop-floor environment, absorbing information almost through his pores to feed the strategic business decisions he will make the next day. [1]

> *'From behind a desk is not the best place to see the world.'*
> Anon.

WHERE SHOULD LEADERS BE? OUT IN THE BUSINESS

- **Feargal Quinn**, the multi-millionaire founder of the Irish supermarket chain *Superquinn*, used to hold meetings with suppliers in the aisles of his supermarkets rather than in an office. The meetings were constantly interrupted by customers coming up to talk to him. 'When I do have the occasional internal meeting in an office with my managers, I often find

I am the most informed person in the room. I tell them things I picked up direct from customers or frontline staff. Their response is often an embarrassed, "Well, we didn't know that,"' he said.

- **Terry Leahy**, CEO of UK supermarket chain *Tesco*, regularly spends a day stacking shelves in one of his branches. He also wanders around rival supermarkets informally.

   In business-to-business organizations it's the same. Tom Peters says the CEOs of *IBM* and other giants spend at least 50 per cent of their time with customers. **Jack Welch**, *General Electric*'s most famous CEO, used to head out of the office and tour the country for a couple of months each year, having lunch with hundreds of customers at each sitting to learn for himself what their issues were. Actually they weren't 'sittings'. They were stand-up buffets where he could keep moving, explained Welch once, because 'you don't want to get cornered at these things.'

- **Mike Rollins**, CEO of *Pizza Hut International*, used to get data sent to him every Friday on the company's most valuable customers. He then called two of them up to talk to them or, as he put it, 'to savour and explore the customer condition'. [2]

- **Richard Branson** was pushing a trolley down the aisle of one of *Virgin*'s Jumbo Jets, serving drinks to passengers. Afterwards he commented to the flight crew how difficult it was not to keep bumping into things and how the trolley blocking the aisle was no fun for passengers. It opened up a conversation that led to the decision to move from trolley service in Upper Class to a more waitress-like service. [3]

- **Jan Carlzon**, turnaround CEO at the airline *SAS*, spent the first couple of weeks in his new job flying as a passenger, hanging around in airport terminal lounges, listening to customers and experiencing what they were experiencing. He took constant notes in a notebook that he carried everywhere. Only then did he step into the boardroom and present the turnaround strategy he had come up with, based on his time immersed in the business. [4]

USEFUL CONCEPT

Close to the customer: In most organizations, distance from the customer denotes seniority. The more contact you have with customers, the lower your status must be (though this is not said openly). Tom Peters and Bob Waterman put customers and the frontline at the heart of the business agenda with the phrase 'close to the customer' in the book *In Search of Excellence* in 1982. A quarter of a century later, many leaders still don't realize that they have to take this phrase literally and spend a significant portion of their time where their business actually is.

SOURCES AND FURTHER READING

(1) *See, Feel, Think, Do: The Power of Instinct in Business,* Andy Milligan and Shaun Smith.

(2) My notes from a talk given by *Yahoo*'s Tim Sanders to the *North American Conference on Customer Management,* Orlando, Florida, November 2003.

(3) *Losing My Virginity,* Richard Branson.

(4) *Moments of Truth,* Jan Carlzon.

A 60 Second Leader Tale: Community of purpose

Leaders don't necessarily instil purpose into people, using a vision and mission. Rather, they tap into a pre-existing, underlying sense of purpose that is part of the human condition, and help people to recognize and articulate it. Here are two *30 Second Leader Tales* illustrating how leaders help people become aware of an existing but perhaps forgotten or unacknowledged unity of purpose, and remind us what we are here for.

PROFESSOR AIDAN HALLIGAN ON THE NHS

'There was a recruitment advertisement placed in *The Times*. It was possibly the most effective recruitment advert in the history of HR. It said this:

> *Men wanted for hazardous journey.*
> *Small wages, bitter cold.*
> *Long hours of complete darkness.*
> *Constant hunger.*
> *Safe return doubtful.*
> *Honour and recognition in the event of success.*

It was the advertisement placed by Shackleton for his Antarctic expedition of 1915. We try and harness people's motivation with visions and missions. But, you can't injunct motivation and harness it to your will. Motivation is intrinsic. When I used to stand up and talk to groups of nurses and doctors about improving the *National Health Service*, there would be a sense of reserve in the audience, perhaps a sense that I was about to add yet more instruction from above to people who are already very stretched.

I often started by reading that advert out to them. Then I'd say "I think that's the reason a lot of us joined the NHS." And they'd laugh out loud. And that's when you know you've connected with them, and you've re-connected them with the selfless reasons many of them joined the *National Health Service*. And they know you share their agenda.'

PROFESSOR JOHN KOTTER ON MATSUSHITA

I heard Professor John Kotter tell this story about the Japanese business leader Matsushita:

'At the end of World War II, Matsushita stood up before a gathering of thousands of his dejected, demoralized workforce, in an occupied country, with all the company's inventory taken by the occupying power, and said, "I've been thinking about purpose."

He then painted a word picture that spoke to everyone, about how taking the lead in quality and innovation and low prices would force competitors to do the same and "in 250 years would eliminate poverty in Japan."'

Author's note: *This, incidentally, was very similar to Sam Walton's stated purpose with Wal-Mart – to bring a wide range of goods only available to the few down in price and into the hands of the mass of ordinary Americans.*

'He sat down to a silence. There was a long pause. Then, one by one, his employees stood up, some with tears in their eyes, and said "I think I could dedicate my life to this." Much of the "Japanese way" that conquered the world's economy in the 1980s can be traced back to that moment.'

SOURCES

(1) Professor Aidan Halligan, in an interview with the author. Professor Halligan was Deputy Chief Medical Officer for England and Director of Clinical Governance for the UK's National Health Service.

(2) Professor John Kotter has written about Matsushita in his biography *Matsushita Leadership*.

24. The 60 Second Leader and …

FRONTLINE LEADERSHIP (2)

Why most leadership fails. Distributed leadership. Go make footprints.

Most leadership thinking is about as useful as a one-legged stool. Because most leadership thinking identifies an organization's leaders as those at the top. The CEO is the main leader. The Executive Board is where some form of group leadership is played out. Heads of Department lead their department.

This is a one-legged framework based purely on position and job title. It can hop up and down, but it's not actually going anywhere. Of course those at the top are in leadership positions; but there are two other widely ignored types of leader in an organization. – and it is only with all three legs in place that any actual leading will get done.

DISTRIBUTED LEADERSHIP

As well as the executive leaders, **Peter Senge**'s research identified internal network leaders and local line leaders. Without these two categories of embedded leaders, new ideas won't get actioned.

In fact, he found '… companies that are able to sustain significant change over many years do so with very little top leader involvement at all. Find the people who are at the heart of the value-generating process – who design, produce, and sell products; who provide services; who talk to customers.' Those are the people who will lead your business where you want it to go.' [1]

COVEY'S BOAT ANALOGY

Stephen Covey [2] describes distributed leadership versus hierarchical leadership as white-water rafting versus rowing in an 'eight'.

Traditional rowing takes place on flat, stable water (the slow-moving, predictable markets of the past). One person steers and dictates the pace in a rigid boat while the other seven just provide the muscle. The crew can't even see where they are going; they're facing the wrong way.

With white-water rafting, one person may be setting the overall direction, but the leadership action takes place all around the edge of a boat that flexes and changes shape as the water (the fast-changing market) swirls and surges around them. The crew's eyes are outward on the market, not turned inward to the 'boss'. And everyone is steering: each uses their paddle to propel and manoeuvre their part of the boat away from the rocks and down the river. Only co-ordinated steering can see the boat safely through. One person alone could never respond to all the forces at the different points of the boat and adapt course and shape in time.

USEFUL CONCEPT

Go make footprints: True leadership only takes place if those at the top realize their job is not to create followers: it's to create more leaders. A friend of mine who devised a new approach to CRM (Customer Relationship Management) in the Norwegian Bank where she works cites her CEO as a great example of an executive leader who creates leaders closer to the front line. 'CRM in banking wasn't really working,' she said. She went to him with the germ of an idea for trying something different, a new approach none of the other banks had tried, which involved reaching a personal agreement between the bank's top 200,000 customers to fill in a 'my life' questionnaire each year in exchange for benefits like preferential interest rates. His answer freed her to be a leader: 'Go make footprints,' he said. And she did. Last I heard, some of the biggest UK retail banks were visiting her to see how she does it.

SOURCES AND FURTHER READING

(1) *The Fifth Discipline*, Peter Senge (get the 2006 edition with the 100 extra pages where he admits some of the weaknesses in his original thesis and learns from organizations that have tried to create a learning organization that harnesses all three types of leader).

(2) *The Seven Habits of Highly Effective People*, Stephen Covey.

A 60 Second Leader Tale: Sam Walton's rules

In his 1992 book *Made in America,* Sam Walton, founder of *Wal-Mart Stores,* Inc., compiled a list of ten key factors known as:

'SAM'S RULES FOR BUILDING A BUSINESS'

- **Rule 1**: Commit to your business. Believe in it more than anybody else. I think I overcame every single one of my personal shortcomings by the sheer passion I brought to my work. I don't know if you're born with this kind of passion, or if you can learn it.

- **Rule 2**: Share your profits with all your Associates, and treat them as partners. In turn, they will treat you as a partner, and together you will all perform beyond your wildest expectations. Remain a corporation and retain control if you like, but behave as a servant leader in a partnership.

- **Rule 3**: Motivate your partners. Money and ownership alone aren't enough. Constantly, day by day, think of new and more interesting ways to motivate and challenge your partners. Set high goals, encourage competition, and then keep score. Make bets with outrageous payoffs.

- **Rule 4**: Communicate everything you possibly can to your partners. The more they know, the more they'll understand. The more they understand, the more they'll care. Once they care, there's no stopping them. If you don't trust your Associates to know what's going on, they'll know you don't really consider them partners.

- **Rule 5**: Appreciate everything your Associates do for the business. A pay check and a stock option will buy one kind of loyalty. But all of us like to be told how much somebody appreciates what we do for them. We like to hear it often, and especially when we have done something we're really proud of.

- **Rule 6**: Celebrate your successes. Find some humor in your failures. Don't take yourself so seriously. Loosen up, and everybody around you will loosen up. Have fun. Show enthusiasm – always. When all else fails, put on a costume and sing a silly song. Then make everybody else sing with you.

- **Rule 7**: Listen to everyone in your company. And figure out ways to get them talking. The folks on the front lines – the ones who actually talk to the customer – are the only ones who really know what's going on out there. You'd better find out what they know.

- **Rule 8**: Exceed your customers' expectations. If you do, they'll come back over and over. Give them what they want – and a little more. Let them know you appreciate them. Make good on all your mistakes, and don't make excuses – apologize. Stand behind everything you do.

- **Rule 9**: Control your expenses better than your competition. This is where you can always find the competitive advantage. For 25 years running – long before Wal-Mart was known as the nation's largest retailer – we ranked No. 1 in our industry for the lowest ratio of expenses to sales.

- **Rule 10**: Swim upstream. Go the other way. Ignore the conventional wisdom. If everybody else is doing it one way, there's a good chance you can find your niche by going in exactly the opposite direction. But be prepared for a lot of folks to wave you down and tell you you're headed the wrong way.

Source: *www.walmart.com.*

GREAT LEADERSHIP

25. The 60 Second Leader and ...

EGO

The problem with heroes. The Icarus paradox. Bad to great?

What's the difference between God and Larry Ellison?
God doesn't think he's Larry Ellison.
Old Silicon Valley joke referring to the immodest boss of *Oracle*

THE PROBLEM WITH HEROES

There's an argument about charisma going on at the moment: specifically, whether it's a good thing to have in a leader. The noisy 'pro' lobby is headed by Tom Peters, who likes to shout a lot (and is usually worth listening to, albeit from a safe distance). The 'anti' lobby is led quietly, as you'd expect, by whispering Jim Collins, author of *Good to Great*.

Peters loves swashbuckling, larger-than-life leaders whose personalities mirror his own. His former student, Collins, holds up as the acme of leadership those ego-lite, selfless 'Level 5' leaders, as he calls them, who happen to be as bookish as he is.

Now it took Peters himself to come up with a delicious insight, which I overheard in a seminar of his I helped organize. He was ranting about how wrong Collins was, when he suddenly paused and said, almost to himself: 'I am increasingly convinced that when writers write, whatever we think we are writing about, we are actually writing about ourselves.' True.

Peter Senge points out that the problem with the 'leader as hero' paradigm, which tends to come with the territory with charismatic leaders, is what happens when they are not around. They put themselves at the centre of the action and always expect to fly in and save the day. [1]

THE ICARUS PARADOX

I think at the root of the argument is a confusion of charisma and ego. Charisma is assumed to embrace brashness, theatricality, basking in the spotlight. Nelson Mandela embraces none of those things, but he is perhaps the most charismatic leader of our generation.

We've all worked with magnetic, compelling people who are charismatic without the ego. But I have to agree with Collins when he says this:

> 'The moment a leader allows himself to become the primary reality people worry about, rather than reality being the primary reality, you have a recipe for mediocrity, or worse.' [2]

The Harvard academic Joseph Baradaccio says this about leaders who court greatness: 'There is a quotation from F. Scott Fitzgerald: "Show me a hero and I'll tell you a tragedy." There's (also) the age-old myth of Icarus trying to fly too close to the sun, and there is the suggestion that there is something dangerous about the pursuit of greatness.' [3]

A 2006 survey helped reconcile the argument about whether ego-heavy or selfless leaders are the most effective. It found that narcissism naturally drives people to seek positions of power and influence, and that therefore you will find more egotists at the top of organizations than among the general population. [4]

As for their performance, egotistical bosses tend to be less self-limiting, as you can imagine, gambling with more resources on their own judgement than less self-regarding leaders. They went in for more and bigger mergers, for example. Their results were consequently more extreme (bigger wins or bigger losses) than their Collins-inspired quiet leader peers. The greater volatility of narcissistic leaders is reflected in greater extremes of good and bad in their financial performance.

BAD TO GREAT?

So can you behave 'badly' – egotists tend to be arbitrary, take the credit and, even Peters admits, can be tyrannical – and still be great? I don't think so.

You need to be able to subordinate your ego to be a great leader. **Stephen Covey** puts it this way:

> *'One area that leaders need to develop to become great leaders is conscience – subordinating yourself. This takes great strength. Both Hitler and Gandhi were people of vision, discipline and passion. The difference was conscience. Anwar Sadat, President of Egypt, vowed never to shake the hands of the Israelis. But, he did just that – subordinating himself – for the sake of peace. When asked why, he said: "He who cannot change the very fabric of his thought will never be able to change reality and will never, therefore, be able to make any progress."'* [5]

SOURCES AND FURTHER READING

(1) *The Fifth Discipline*, Peter Senge.

(2) *www.JimCollins.com.*

(3) *Leading Quietly: An Unorthodox Guide to Doing The Right Thing*, Joseph Baradaccio.

(4) *It's All About Me*, a study presented to the 2006 gathering of the *American Academy of Management* by Arijit Chatterjee and Donald Hambrick of Pennsylvania State University.

(5) Stephen Covey was talking at a conference I helped organize, the *European Conference on Customer Management*, in London in 2002. On the other hand, there is the 'Hitler's ghost' argument, which Barbara Kellerman puts forward in her book *Bad Leadership*. You need to distinguish between bad as in 'ineffective' and bad as in 'unethical', argues Kellerman, pointing out that Hitler was hardly an ineffective leader. I would argue, though, that few would call Hitler a 'great' leader. 'Great' is implicitly approving, with its meaning grounded in Aristotle's definition of greatness as leading a life characterized by a number of virtues (see Chapter 26, *Humility*). Therefore, the word 'great' doesn't fit when applied to highly effective but unethical leaders.

A 60 Second Leader Tale: Who's more important: you or me?

Horst Schulze is the inspiring founder and first President of the *Ritz-Carlton* hotel chain. I heard him once explain how leaders need to put their own ego in their pocket and make it clear to the people who do the work that *they* are the mission critical people and the leader's job is just to support them:

'At every new hotel, I gave the orientation myself. I have done it at 45 hotels so far. From the busboy to the housekeepers to the room service chefs, I line up the new hires and say to them one important question: "Who's more important to this hotel: you or me?"

I then tell them: "It's you! If I don't go to work on Monday morning, nobody knows. Nobody cares. If you don't, the food doesn't get served, the beds don't get made. **You are far more important than me!**"'

Schulze also paid far more attention to the recruitment and job profiling process than his competitors in the hotel industry:

'After induction, the next step is to orientate them to **who we are** so they can become **part of** the company, not just work **for** the company. This applies to everyone, even, say, dishwashers. I have only ever fired three General Managers. One of them was a man who said to me, "You want to give a dishwasher a process?" as if a dishwasher is beneath having a process. How arrogant of him!'

Schulze completed the recruitment, induction and training process with a third creative leadership step: 'So after hiring and orientation you have training. Here's something powerful and simple that we do: *The best room service waiters write the training manual for the new room service waiters*,' he said.

The *Ritz-Carlton* chain became legendary for the quality of its service, which Schulze puts down to the way initiative and decision-making is pushed down to the frontline employees. Even bellboys have the power to spend up to $2,000 of company money to put right a customer complaint or unexpected problem, without having to ask permission.

26. The 60 Second Leader and ...

HUMILITY

Weak is the new strong. A community of purpose. The qualities of greatness.

> 'We have come to see leadership as being about one person, whereas really it is about the actions that people take.'
> Professor John Kotter
>
> 'The idea that leadership is about one person with a vision and mission who will figure out for the organization the best process and structure is simply not true ... Leadership does not have to be centred around one person or a small group.'
> Ricardo Semler, *Semco SA*

WEAK IS THE NEW STRONG

Leadership, as with everything else in life today, is increasingly about embracing paradox – thinking *and* rather than *or*. In the case of leadership, the most difficult paradox for many is that you have to serve to lead. [1]

Strong leadership today often involves a clarification and harnessing of the collective will, and a determination to serve it, rather than the dominance of an individual will over the collective. As we have seen in the previous chapter, strong leadership often demands the suppression of the formal leader's ego rather than its expression.

A COMMUNITY OF PURPOSE

The very concept of leadership has had to adapt to the emergence of a self-aware, increasingly self-directed workforce with a strong need for meaning and, for many, a desire to be part of *a community of purpose*. With questioning, self-aware, wised-up people, instruction from above will deliver at best compliance (if you are lucky), but not commitment.

There is a second, structural reason why traditional ideas of strong leadership, in which the leader expresses his or her will and followers carry it out, are now inadequate. In flatter organizations, where leadership is to some degree decentralized, people are expected to step up and lead when required. They are not leaders all of the time. Hence, when taking the lead on a particular issue, they do not speak to each other from a position of formal authority. So instructive leadership based on position has to give way to something else.

THE QUALITIES OF GREAT LEADERSHIP

To find this 'something else' – this expanded sense of leadership – I think we need to look back to move forward. The philosopher and author **Tom Morris** holds up as a model the **Aristotlean** virtues of leadership. [2] Tom lists them as:

- Courage
- Temperance
- Liberality
- Magnificence
- Pride
- Good temper
- Friendliness
- Truthfulness
- Wittiness
- Justice.

Temperance equates to conscience and self-control. *Liberality* moves us away from a reliance on rules and delivers the ability to flex, based on trusting the good sense of colleagues and a common direction and code of conduct. *Magnificence* equates to generosity of spirit and performance enhancement, the ability to *magnify* one's own and others' performance. In recent leadership jargon, *magnificence* would equate to transformational leadership; the ability to inspire extraordinary performance from ordinary people.

How many corporate CEOs could you tick off all ten of those qualities against? But, that question slides past the more important point. The great thing about the Aristotlean virtues as a rule of thumb for great leadership is that they apply to all levels of the organization. How great would your leadership culture be if everyone were held to account against those ten virtues? Acts of leadership from all corners of the organization is what you would get.

USEFUL CONCEPT

Strong opinions, weakly held: If you are too attached to your own view, you can't see or hear evidence that clashes with it. You will be blind-sided by markets that move in a direction you had failed to anticipate, and surrounded by weak minds who are afraid to challenge you. The *Palo Alto Institute For the Future* advises leaders to have '*strong opinions, weakly held*'. A leader from the recent past, **Larry Bossidy**, former Chairman of *Honeywell*, says something similar: 'Maintain your values and ethics for a lifetime, but don't be afraid to change your opinions. That's where self-renewal comes from. It was Jack Welch's great secret.'

SOURCES AND FURTHER READING

(1) See the many books on **servant leadership**, a phrase coined by **Robert Greenleaf,** and Chapter 28, *Love,* in this book. **Ken Blanchard** is perhaps the most popular proponent of servant leadership. Nelson Mandela's first words to the microphone from a balcony, speaking to a massed crowd, on being released after 24 years in Robben Island, were: 'I stand here not as a prophet, but as a humble servant of you, the people.' Perhaps the most powerful three-word expression of servant-leadership – in the sense of leaders not being separate from the people they serve – is from the US Constitution. It is simply this: 'We, the people …'

(2) *If Aristotle Ran General Motors*, Tom Morris.

A 60 Second Leader Tale: Gorbachev and humility

I'm convinced you get glimpses of true leadership in the personal anecdotes people tell rather than in official stories. Every first-hand anecdote I've heard about **Mikhail Gorbachev** reinforces what an exceptional leader he was, despite the way he is vilified today within Russia.

Here are three true, personal, first-hand tales of Gorbachev; one I heard from **General Colin Powell**, the other two from leadership guru **Rene Carayol**. Powell's story shows how you can show humility – asking for help and admitting the Cold War is effectively lost, as Gorbachev was doing in this case – without being weak. It actually takes great strength to reveal vulnerability rather than hide it behind aggression. Gorbachev is assertive and displays powerful leadership, disarming Powell and winning him over.

WHEN POWELL MET GORBACHEV [1]

'I remember going to see President Gorbachev when he was leading his country through *perestroika* and *glasnost*. He said to me "You are not doing enough to help! You know what we are trying to do here and you need to help us do it!" I sat back and made it clear that, well, he was still a Commie, I guess, and the USSR had been the enemy for decades. He leant forward and smiled. "Mr. Secretary," he said, "I am afraid you will need to find yourself a new enemy."' [1]

WHEN CARAYOL MET GORBACHEV [2]

'I was part of an event where Gorbachev was due to speak. This was in the days when Raisa, his wife, was still alive. They were, you will remember, devoted to each other. He was sitting next to her at a table. It was a very high-powered meeting.

When it was his turn to speak, he rose, looking a little tense, but Raisa touched his hand. He looked down at her; she said something to him. He seemed to relax, smiled and went over to the lectern. I couldn't resist sidling over to his interpreter and asking what she had said. "She said, 'You will be fine. It will be OK.'" he said.

This man had changed the course of history, had faced down some of the most reactionary power bases in the world, had put in motion forces that had led to the Berlin wall tumbling. Outside Russia he is recognized as a world statesman of great bravery and stature. Yet he was nervous about talking to this gathering of people in a room. It was a nice reminder that brave leaders aren't fearless, they just conquer that fear; in this case, with a little help.'

WHEN CARAYOL MET GORBACHEV A SECOND TIME [3]

'Great leaders are clear what they stand for. I asked Gorbachev what he stood for as a leader. He answered: "Making people happy and giving them the space and opportunity to establish their dreams."

We then had lunch, where his daughter Irina translated for us. I told him over lunch, "I have a daughter, too. She is sixteen." Which means, I explained, that when she was being born, his Russia was giving birth to *glasnost* and *perestroika*. If our child was a boy, we were going to call him Mikhail in his honour, I explained. As we couldn't call her Mikhail, we named her Raisa, after his wife (who had died a few years previously). Even today, our daughter Raisa's nickname is still Gorby, I told him.

He stood up, with a tear in his eye and gave me a bear hug. That's a true anecdote, but the real story it illuminates is that great leaders have humility. They have the grand sweep of view and self-belief that a leader needs, but combined with the intimacy of connection with individuals and a humble sense of themselves as a person.

Self-belief and humility: These are the two qualities all great leaders share.'

SOURCES

(1) I heard General Colin Powell tell this Gorbachev story at *Leaders in London,* November 2006. Powell was Secretary of State at the time of the encounter.

(2) Leadership guru Rene Carayol, talking at an *Inspired Leaders Network* event. Rene has a way of seeing past the public face of leadership and spotting the intimate detail that brings an insight into what leadership really is, as you can see from these two true tales of his. Here's his website if you want to subscribe to his newsletter. I recommend it: *www.carayol.com.*

(3) Rene Carayol in an interview with the author after he had chaired *Leaders in London 2005,* where Gorbachev was one of the main guests.

27. The 60 Second Leader and ...

FEAR

What people fear. When John Kotter was scared. The opposite of fear.

In a Canadian poll probing irrational anxieties, pollster Allan Gregg asked, 'If someone told you something was safe and someone else told you it was unsafe, which one would you believe?' He found that an astounding '68 per cent would accept the message of doom and gloom' without questioning who was telling them and what they were talking about. [1]

WHAT PEOPLE FEAR

People are fearful of change. The primitive part of our brain, the amygdala, associates change with the unknown and so reacts to it with caution, fear and fear's manifestation, aggression. The need to be in control and to dominate is a common expression of fear.

Even great leaders feel fear, despite appearances to the contrary. '*I was scared to death. It was terrifying. I literally had nightmares.* I was supposed to be director of engineering, but there were so few of us that they made me director of operations,' [2] said *Intel* employee No. 3, Andy Grove, who had to teach himself how to morph from engineer to leader. Grove is now one of America's most admired business leaders.

By contrast, '*The rest of us live in fear. Walt had no fear,*' says Disney historian Jim Korkis. I would have to respectfully disagree with Korkis. People with no fear are reckless. My reading of Disney is that his belief in the possible was so much larger than other people that it overcame his fear – fear of failure, of letting others down, particularly his employees when money was tight in *Disney*'s early days.

WHEN JOHN KOTTER WAS SCARED

Even leadership gurus get scared. I came across this humble admission from John Kotter in an interview on leadership, after Kotter had answered a question by saying that leaders have to overcome their own fear: [3]

Q: Has there been a time in your life that you've had to overcome a fear in order to get to where you wanted to go?

JK: Oh, yeah! Not only one time. Good heavens! At one point, I had an extraordinarily difficult boss who could literally drive you to tears. And it was easy to convince yourself to allow the fear that naturally arose to, if not paralyze you, certainly greatly restrict what you did, and the risks you were willing to take. And I think coming to grips with that was not an easy one.

Q: Were you able to face your fear?

JK: I decided life was too short to hide in the corner and worry about this guy. And I also decided that I was right, and he wasn't.

Q: Did you tell him that?

JK: Did I ever tell him that? I may not have …

USEFUL CONCEPT

The opposite of fear is … trust, or sometimes love. When you trust your own abilities and those of the people around you, you overcome fear. And when the people you lead trust themselves and you – trust that you have their best interests at heart and are authentic – that is when you and they will achieve the most. When you love you reveal vulnerabilities instead of hiding them through fear. In that sense, love liberates from fear – hence the title of the next chapter.

Warren Bennis – still, for me, the most insightful thinker on leadership I have ever met – talks about how adversity forges resilience. *Resilience* is a wonderful and underused word in recruitment advertisements and job specifications, incidentally. Evidence of resilience is one of the primary requirements you should be looking for in people at all levels. Warren says that, if you look back, you will find that great leaders have commonly been through one or more major difficulties in their life and that they were, essentially, forged in the heat of that crucible – that they emerged stronger as a leader.

You don't necessarily have to have overcome those challenges, either. Being broken by circumstance and coming back from that can leave you less fearful too. As Hemingway observed: 'The world breaks everyone and afterward some are strong at the broken places.'

The same is true of fear of failure. Once you have failed and know it doesn't destroy you, you can choose to get up and try again. And so we come full circle to the subject that starts this book. As Churchill so memorably said, success consists of being able to go from failure to failure without loss of enthusiasm.

TAKE THEM TO THE EDGE

When I'm thinking about this subject, I find I constantly return to this poem by Christopher Logue. It reminds me that overcoming fear – in yourself and others – is one of the fundamentals of great leadership. This is the real dialogue that goes on between a leader and the people he or she leads:

Come to the edge.
We might fall.
Come to the edge.
It is too high.
Come to the edge.
And they came,
and he pushed,
and they flew. [4]

SOURCES AND FURTHER READING

(1) *The Leader's Digest*, Jim Clemmer.

(2) *Andy Grove: The Life and Times of an American*, Richard Tedlow.

(3) *www.business-marketing.com* (click on 'articles' in the menu).

(4) Christopher Logue, written as a poster for an exhibition celebrating the poet Guillaume Apollinaire, who is often wrongly said to be the poem's author.

A 60 Second Leader Tale: 'You are capable of great things'

These three 20 Second Tales from **Richard Branson** illustrate how people can be challenged through *Love* (Chapter 28) to overcome *Fear* (see above) and achieve great things.

I was talking to Elizabeth Handy, wife of Charles Handy, on the phone recently (name dropper? *Moi?*). She reminded me of a point in Handy's book, *The Alchemists*. 'People who achieve great things were usually told when they were a child, by an adult who believed it, that they were capable of great things,' she said. It applies to adults, too, of course.

I once asked a friend of mine who is a manager at *Virgin Atlantic*, 'So, from the point of view of someone who works for him, is he really a great leader?' 'Yes. No question,' she answered. 'And his mum is the reason he is the way he is.' I didn't understand what she meant until I came across this story. Here's how Branson's mum let him discover he was capable of great things:

---

1   MAKE YOUR OWN WAY HOME, RICKY

'When I was four years old, Mum stopped the car a few miles from our house and told me to find my own way home across the fields. She made it a game, one I was happy to play. It was an early challenge.

As I grew older, these lessons grew harder. Early one winter morning, Mum shook me awake and told me to get dressed. It was dark and cold, but I crawled out of bed. I was given a packed lunch and an apple. "I'm sure you'll find some water along the way," Mum said, as she waved me off on a fifty-mile bike ride to the south coast.

It was still dark when I set off on my own. I spent the night with a relative and returned home the next day. When I walked into the kitchen at home, I felt very proud. I was sure I would be greeted with cheers. Instead, Mum said, "Well done, Ricky. Was that fun? Now run along – the vicar wants you to chop some logs for him."

> To some people this might sound harsh. But the members of my family love and care for each other very much. We are a close-knit unit. My parents wanted us to be strong and to rely on ourselves.'

Now, spot the connection between that and the way Branson encourages his people to believe in themselves:

---

2   INSPIRE PEOPLE TO BELIEVE THEY CAN DO GREAT THINGS TOO

'One of the things I try and do at *Virgin* is make people think about themselves and see themselves more positively. I firmly believe that anything is possible. I tell them, "Believe in yourself. You can do it." I also say, "Be bold, but don't gamble."'

You can see how that 'Find your own way home, Ricky' spirit fostered by Branson's mum helped to shape Branson as he grew older, in this final tale:

---

3   HOW TO START AN AIRLINE

'Our plan was to travel on to Puerto Rico – but when we got to the airport, the flight was cancelled. People were roaming about, looking lost. No one was doing anything. So I did – someone had to.

I made some calls and chartered a plane for about $2,000. I divided that by the number of people. It came to $39 a head. I borrowed a blackboard and wrote on it:

VIRGIN AIRWAYS. $39 SINGLE FLIGHT TO PUERTO RICO

… I had never chartered a plane before.'

So, you can trace the 'can-do' attitude that Branson has infected his Virgin companies with all the way back to that four-year-old who was challenged to find his own way home.

Source: These three stories are from Richard Branson's short book *Screw It, Let's Do It*, which is a cut-down version of his autobiography *Losing My Virginity*.

28. The 60 Second Leader and ...

LOVE

What's love got to do with it? Love is ...

> *'I would far rather have a business led by love than by fear.'*
> Herb Kelleher, *Southwest Airlines*
>
> *'... whether it is better to be loved or feared? The answer is that one would like to be both; but because it is difficult to combine them, it is far better to be feared than loved.'*
> Niccolo Machiavelli, *The Prince*

'It might sound slightly bizarre,' says **Ken Blanchard**, co-author of *The One Minute Manager,* 'but one of the key beliefs for effective leadership is to be madly in love with all the people you are leading.'

Well, you are right, Ken. It does sound slightly bizarre. For many managers, leadership is the love that dare not speak its name.

Having said that, a surprising number of hard-nosed leaders are unafraid to talk about love as being fundamental to leadership. **Rudy Giuliani**, the former Mayor of New York, tells us there are three keys to leadership:

1   If you are going to lead, be optimistic. If you're not, your followers can hardly be expected to be.

2   If you don't love people, do something else.

3   Be absolutely clear what you stand for. [1]

LOVE IS ...

A definition would help ease any discomfort you might be feeling. **Tim Collins**, a career soldier, rose to prominence when an impromptu speech he gave to the Irish regiment he commanded in Iraq ended up in newspapers all over the world. Collins says, like Kelleher, Giuliani and Blanchard, that 'to lead effectively, you have to love people'. Collins goes on to explain 'love' as knowing and caring about what motivates people and what is important to them, and helping them fulfil those aspirations at work. This, he says, is a foundation of leadership. [2]

Fear constrains behaviour; love liberates it. So, if all you need is compliance, fear will probably do. But fear freezes initiative, stifles creativity, and provides no incentive to stretch and grow. Love is about wanting and allowing people to be at their best, and engaging with them to help them achieve that. 'Love is the selfless promotion of the growth of the other,' is **Milton Mayeroff**'s definition. [3]

Sharing knowledge, looking after employees' well-being, giving people your time and attention, respecting and acknowledging the contribution of others, all are incontrovertible aspects of good leadership. It only becomes controversial when the 'L' word is applied.

Jim Clemmer, a Canadian leadership thinker I admire, gets to the heart of the matter with this insight: 'Leadership is emotional. Leadership deals with feelings. Leadership is made up of dreams, inspiration, excitement, desire, pride, care, passion, and love. The areas of our lives where we show the strongest leadership – including our communities, families, organizations, products, services, hobbies, and customers – are where we're most in love.' [4]

I think even the most emotionally reserved leader can, at a push, understand the definition of love put forward by Colonel Collins, above. But, being 'in love' or even 'madly in love', as Clemmer and Blanchard put it, is still a step too far for many managers.

USEFUL CONCEPT

Transformational versus transactional leadership: 'I ask people all the time, "Would you rather be magnificent or ordinary at work?" Everyone chooses magnificent. I don't get anyone choosing ordinary. And yet, do we regularly get magnificent behaviour at work? No we don't. I think that's because of the way we treat people.' In that quote, Ken Blanchard is explaining how a transformational leader works, and that requires love. If you are purely a transactional leader – negotiating performance in return for a material reward – love is not necessary, some would argue. Equally, however, ordinary people are unlikely to be inspired to extraordinary performance levels by transactional leadership alone.

SOURCES AND FURTHER READING

(1) *Leadership*, Rudy Giuliani.

(2) My notes from a speech given by Tim Collins at the end of November 2006.

(3) *Love is the Killer App*, Tim Sanders.

(4) *www.clemmer.net.*

See also: *Primal Leadership*, Daniel Goleman *et al.*, and Goleman's other books on emotional intelligence.

A 60 Second Leader Tale: Lead like Walt

Here are eight mini-tales about Walt Disney, from people who knew him. Each one illustrates a learning point from one or more chapters in this book.

---

1 CONNECT: LEADERSHIP IS PERSONAL

'Whenever anyone called him "Mr. Disney" he got upset. It was always Walt. And he always knew your name. In the early days, we didn't wear nametags, but Walt still called you by your first name. Once he knew your name, he never forgot it.'

Gary Carlson, *Disney* Sound Engineer

2 ACTION AND HUMILITY: LEADERS LEAD BY EXAMPLE

Journalist Art Linkletter turned up for a screening of Disney's new movie *Fantasia*. He arrived early for the press conference and found the place empty except for one fellow who was busily arranging chairs.

'I said, "When is Walt Disney supposed to arrive?"

He grinned and said, "I'm Walt Disney."

I said, "You are? Why are you arranging chairs?"

"Well," he said, "I like to have things just-so."'

3 CHALLENGE: GET PEOPLE TO BELIEVE THEY ARE CAPABLE OF MORE

'Walt had more confidence in us as artists than we had in ourselves. I'm a sculptor now, but I used to be an animator, and I loved it. I didn't want to leave animation and go work in the theme parks. But Walt saw me as a sculptor and he sold me on it. He made me believe I could do it. He gave us the confidence to do things we never imagined were possible.'

Blaine Gibson, *Disney* sculptor

4   STRATEGY: FIRST, BREAK ALL THE SECTORAL RULES

'Today you hear people talk about "thinking outside the box". But Walt would say, "No! Don't think outside the box! Once you say that, you've established that there is a box." Walt would refuse to accept the existence of the box.'

Disney historian Jim Korkis

5   EXECUTION: MAKE YOUR UNIQUE STRATEGY A REALITY

Walt Disney died before *Disney World* in Florida could be completed. On opening day in 1971, almost five years after his death, someone commented to Mike Vance, creative director of *Walt Disney Studios*, 'Isn't it too bad Walt Disney didn't live to see this?' 'He did see it,' Vance replied simply. 'That's why it's here.'

6   RAISING PERFORMANCE: DON'T MOTIVATE; INSPIRE

'Walt challenged and inspired you by talking to you. He wouldn't give you detailed instructions about what he wanted you to do. Instead, he would simply point you in the direction he wanted you to go, then leave the rest up to you. He would get you started on the creative process and inspire you with confidence. As a result, you would go far beyond what you thought you were capable of doing.'

Band leader Tutti Camarata, whom Disney recruited to set up *Disneyland Records* (now called *Walt Disney Records*)

7   TEACH: ACTIVELY CONTRIBUTE TO OTHER PEOPLE'S DEVELOPMENT

'Walt ran the studio like a university. We were learning all the time and a few of us were going to art school at night. Walt would drive us there and pick us up later.'

Les Clark, *Disney* animator

8   OVERCOME FEAR – AND SHOW PEOPLE BY EXAMPLE THAT THEY CAN, TOO

'The rest of us live in fear. Walt had no fear.'*

Jim Korkis, *Disney* historian

FURTHER READING

There are a lot of books on Disney, but the one that gives you the most insight into Walt Disney himself, in my view, is *How To Be Like Walt*, by Pat Williams with Jim Denney.

---

*I don't actually agree with Jim Korkis here, but Disney did show people how to act *as if* they had no fear. See Chapter 27, *Fear*, for more on leadership and fear.

29. The 60 Second Leader and ...

PRESENCE

What comes next? Your leadership challenge

The previous few chapters have been hinting that we need to expand the definition of leadership. We have established that 'leadership' is more useful to focus on as a discipline than 'leaders' and that a vibrant organization is full of acts of leadership. I want to take us back to the idea of emergence; that leadership needs to emerge from within complex networks and organizations. The Net gives us an idea of where we are heading.

LEADERSHIP DENIAL

On the Net, leadership denial is everywhere. Network leaders in any community of purpose that has formed itself on the Net are self-consciously *not* leaders. They are go-to people, opinion formers, trend-setters, guides, recruiters of new members, catalysts, the hub around which the action revolves. But they won't call themselves 'leaders'.

There is more than a slug of self-deception mixed into this self-view of those who form and join communities on the Net, but a shared reality is a shared reality. And, as has been wisely noted, **Web 2.0** is really much bigger than that. It is **World 2.0**. The networked world does not live firewalled behind the screen of your laptop. The edges between the Net world and the real world are increasingly blurred. [1]

Sharon Daloz Parks has coined a useful phrase, *Leadership for the new commons,* [2] which helps us focus in on the transfer of power to the 'commons' through the growth of networks. These networks then voluntarily cede that power – often temporarily – to unofficial leaders. This use of the word 'commons' builds on the work of **Lawrence Lessig**. [3]

YOUR LEADERSHIP CHALLENGE

Daloz Parks' start point is that traditional ideas of formal leadership are increasingly inadequate to describe what is going on in our organizations – and what is struggling to emerge. She says, powerfully:

'... those who would lead are always swept up in complex systems larger than themselves. We cannot control but we can creatively intervene in these systems, offering acts of leadership – sometimes going beyond our authorization.'

She then frames the evolution of leadership in the context of Personality vs. Presence.

PERSONALITY VS. PRESENCE

'When the focus shifts from authority and technical problems to leadership and adaptive challenges, the charisma and traits of the individual personality may become less critical. In this view, acts of leadership depend less on the magnetism and social dominance of heroic individuals and more on the capacities of individuals (who may be located in a wide variety of positions) to intervene skillfully in complex systems.'

We are talking adaptive leadership here. **Betty Sue Flowers**, in the book *Presence,* [4] helps us further by outlining the need for a new definition of 'great leadership' in which ordinary people contribute to the creation of extraordinary performance:

'One of the roadblocks for groups moving forward now is thinking that they have to wait for a leader to emerge – someone who embodies the future path. But I think what we've been learning ... is that the future can emerge within the group itself, not embodied in a "hero" or traditional "leader." ... we have to nurture a new form of leadership that doesn't depend on extraordinary individuals.' [5]

She also argues that the role of formal leaders then morphs into one adopted by the ancient Greeks and Chinese, suggesting we need to revive

'The old idea that those in positions to influence such organizations' power must be committed to cultivation or moral development.' Formal leaders then become philosopher-leaders, if you will, helping articulate the ethos of the organization. We have a way to go, she says, because '… our leaders are more likely to be technologists than philosophers, focused on gaining and using power, driving change, influencing people and maintaining an appearance of control.'

USEFUL CONCEPT

Presencing: The idea of *Presencing*, as Peter Senge and his colleagues call it, centres on the assumption that formal leaders are not problem-solvers and decision-makers separate from the change issues they are trying to tackle. Human communities that are aligned behind a common purpose sense their future and act to create it together.

SOURCES AND FURTHER READING

(1) Google this: *Why Things Matter – a 'Manifesto for Networked Objects'*, by Julian Bleeker.

(2) I have hijacked Sharon Daloz Parks's phrase and applied it to a different context from the one she originally created it to describe. See her work for the *Whidbey Institute* at *www.whidbeyinstitute.org*.

(3) *The Future of Ideas: The Fate of the Commons in a Connected World*, Lawrence Lessig.

(4) *Presence: Exploring Profound Change in People, Organizations and Society*, Peter Senge, C. Otto Schwarmer, Joseph Jaworski and Betty Sue Flowers.

(5) Flowers prefaces that with 'The idea that we are experiencing a crisis in leadership probably isn't new, but … If we are at the end of an era, I think it's clear that a new kind of leadership is called for.'

A 60 Second Leader Tale: When the boss disappeared

'For a man who is never far from one of his two mobile phones, **Philip Green** *was unusually hard to get hold of last Wednesday. Little wonder – the billionaire had hidden himself away to call every one of the 67 members of Arcadia's scholarship programme. Six months ago, these lucky things were taken on by Green in a sort of grown-up, real-life version of* The Apprentice. *With half the programme done, Green thought he would give them the gentle, personal touch. Nice. All are staying with Arcadia, but the top 20 will compete for four head-office jobs.'*
The *Sunday Times* newspaper, London

Three quick leader learning points about leaders and people development:

1. How important would you feel if you answered the phone and on the other end was a billionaire you had only seen in the newspapers and on TV – your boss's boss's boss's boss's boss – asking if you have five minutes because he wants to chat about how you are doing on the company scholarship course? He asks what you think of it so far, congratulates you on getting halfway through it, asks if he can help with anything, and then encourages you to get the most out of the second half of the scholarship. How would that sense of importance help form your own idea of leadership and your own behaviour later in your career?

2. If Philip Green can clear his diary to personally coach his rising talent, how much time do you or the bosses in your organization spend on developing other people? Too busy? It's the job of HR? It's not actually. It's the job of existing leaders, with the help of HR, to develop other leaders.

3. **Jack Welch** (then CEO of *GE*) and Herb Kelleher (then CEO of *Southwest Airlines*) spent 40–50 days a year developing people, teaching them their leadership point of view and taking responsibility for their development personally. Welch personally led classes at GE's executive university on a regular basis. How much time do you or the bosses in your organization spend per week, per month, per year, personally developing people? Yes, well spotted: this is the same point as (2). It's so important it needs repeating. Leadership is viral. Leaders don't create followers. They create more leaders.

30. The 60 Second Leader and ...

LEGACY

Leaders don't create followers. They create more leaders.

> *'I was shocked to find that I no longer believe in business education.'*
> Charles Handy

Kamenev and Zinoviev were two Bolshevik leaders under Lenin. The impression Lenin made on them was so great that they both developed his handwriting. Marty Sklar was one of Walt Disney's right-hand men and became Chief Imagineer for the *Disney Corporation*. Walt always used a red pen to make notes. Long after Walt's death, handwritten red notes were still being passed around the Imagineer department, because Sklar would only use a red pen. At *Disney*, when casting around for a creative solution, the question everyone uses, even now, is 'What would Walt do?'

The imprint leaders leave on people is mysterious and the legacy of effective leaders runs deep. But one thing it is not is standardized. HR departments in large organizations that are currently working away diligently on your standardized leadership behaviours, and leadership development systems based on them, please note this.

THERE IS NO 'GREAT LEADER' TEMPLATE

I heard the leadership consultant Rene Carayol put it this way: 'We have been told for years now that there is a standard, homogenized great leader type or template we have to aspire to. Organizations deliver one training programme; people are expected to become clone leaders. That doesn't work. The marketplace tells us that difference works. Challenging the status quo and standing out from the pack is what makes a great leader.'

TOO MUCH THE SAME

If you systematize anything you end up with too much similarity. And that applies to the way large organizations develop leaders. There is already too much sameness out there. Take this example from the maverick business leader Ricardo Semler, who sometimes teaches at *Harvard*: 'I ran an exercise with forty-three *Fortune 500* CEOs. I got them to write down their company values on a piece of card. Then, when they were at coffee, I swapped all the cards around without telling them. When they came back it took them a while to figure out that they had somebody else's values in front of them. They were all saying the same thing.'

LEADERSHIP IS SITUATIONAL

People need to be allowed to develop their own authentic leadership style rather than being developed and assessed according to a rigid interpretation of desired leadership behaviours. As former Secretary of State Colin Powell says: 'Management may be a science. But, leadership is an art. I have never yet seen an environment where you can be a consistent Type A or Type B leader. No one way is right. Different situations call for different types of leadership.'

CEOS DO IT

Large organizations trying to tackle the issue of legacy – growing a cadre of leaders to take over from the current leadership – will find they only really succeed if the CEO and other formal leaders are actively involved in a hands-on way. When top management commit time and energy to the development of leadership is when it is taken seriously by those involved. [1] Also, best-practice companies tend to use fewer competencies in their leadership development models, feeling that simplicity and focus are strong advantages. [2]

If you are involved in developing leaders you also need to know that your development programme has to be focussed on 'doing' not on 'knowing'; it has to be designed expressly to stimulate action that directly benefits the performance of the organization. Leadership development has to be derived directly from the organization's strategy and revolve around real issues. The ideal approach is developing-while-doing.

Finally, get people to manage their leadership development in short, focussed chunks of time – say regular daily or weekly 10–15 minute bursts – that are part of the working week and link to their actual leadership activities, rather than just relying on traditional seminars, retreats or other events that take people away from work for long periods. [3]

Developing leadership isn't a luxury. It's a strategic necessity. I've put together further thoughts to help you build a leadership development process, in a paper that you can request from the website *www.60SecondLeader. com*. You will find a number of leadership resources there, too, to help you take things further. Hope to meet you there.

SOURCES AND FURTHER READING

(1) *The Leadership Investment. How the World's Best Organizations Gain Strategic Advantage Through Leadership Development,* Robert M. Fulmer and Marshall Goldsmith.

(2) *Growing Your Company's Leaders,* Robert Fulmer, Jay Conger.

(3) The work of David Rock, Jeffrey Schwartz and others into how the brain processes information, changes to accept or adapt it, and how that is connected with shifts in behaviour, suggests regular short high-attention activities are more effective.

A Final 60 Second Leader Tale: Herb Kelleher on leaving a legacy

In his final remarks in his *Message to the Field* a few years ago, Herb Kelleher told *Southwest* employees this:

'When you're sitting around with your grandchildren, I want you to be able to tell them that being connected to Southwest Airlines was one of the finest things that ever happened in your entire life. I want you to be able to say, "Southwest Airlines ennobled and enriched my life; it made me better, and bigger, and stronger than I ever could have been alone." And if, indeed, that happens with your grandchildren, then that will be the greatest contribution that I could have made to Southwest Airlines and to its future.'

Source: Kevin and Jackie Freiberg's great book, *Nuts! Southwest Airlines' Crazy Recipe for Business and Personal Success*. So, that's what Kelleher means by 'a company led by love'. Pretty compelling stuff, I'd say ...

WHERE NEXT?

Well, I hate to spoil that little buzz of satisfaction you get from finishing a book, but if *The 60 Second Leader* has inspired you to want to increase your leadership effectiveness – and the leadership of those around you – then the first thing I would advise you to do is ... go back to the beginning and read it again.

Not all at once. Put into practice the advice in Chapter 30, *Legacy*: the latest research into the neuroscience of leadership says we put learning into action more effectively if we focus in regular 10–15 minute sessions.

That is just the right amount of time in which to read one chapter of this book, reflect on one thing you will do differently, then start doing it. Do that daily or weekly (depending on how impatient and driven you are) and, pretty soon, you will have made thirty significant changes in how you lead; changes in fundamental areas of leadership, from decision-making to strategy formation to people motivation. And if you need some peer assistance, join the online community.

HUNGRY FOR MORE?

There are some fundamental questions that can't be answered in a book: 'What kind of leader are you?' 'What kind of leadership culture does your organization have now?' and 'What does it need to do to improve it?'

I have developed some online tools to help you steer a path forward in the development of your own and your organization's leadership, using the same principle of low time investment, high-impact learning that underpins this book. You will find them, and me, in the 60 Second Leader online community on www.60SecondLeader.com. Hope to see you there.

INDEX